As the creator of 'Fierce Females: 40 Empowering Women Portraits to Color and Celebrate,' I'm thrilled to share this collection of inspiring and bold portraits with women everywhere. Each picture was carefully crafted to celebrate the strength and power of women, and I hope that coloring these pages will remind you of your power and potential.

As you color, I encourage your creativity and imagination to run wild. There are no rules or limits when expressing yourself through color, so don't be afraid to experiment and try new things. Let your unique style shine through, whether you choose bold and vibrant colors or more muted and calming hues.

Finally, I want to remind you to celebrate the fierce females in your life, whether it's your mom, sister, friend, or yourself. We all have a strength within us that deserves to be recognized and celebrated, and I hope that this coloring book can serve as a daily reminder of that."

Ava Artflow

This Book Belongs To:

_____

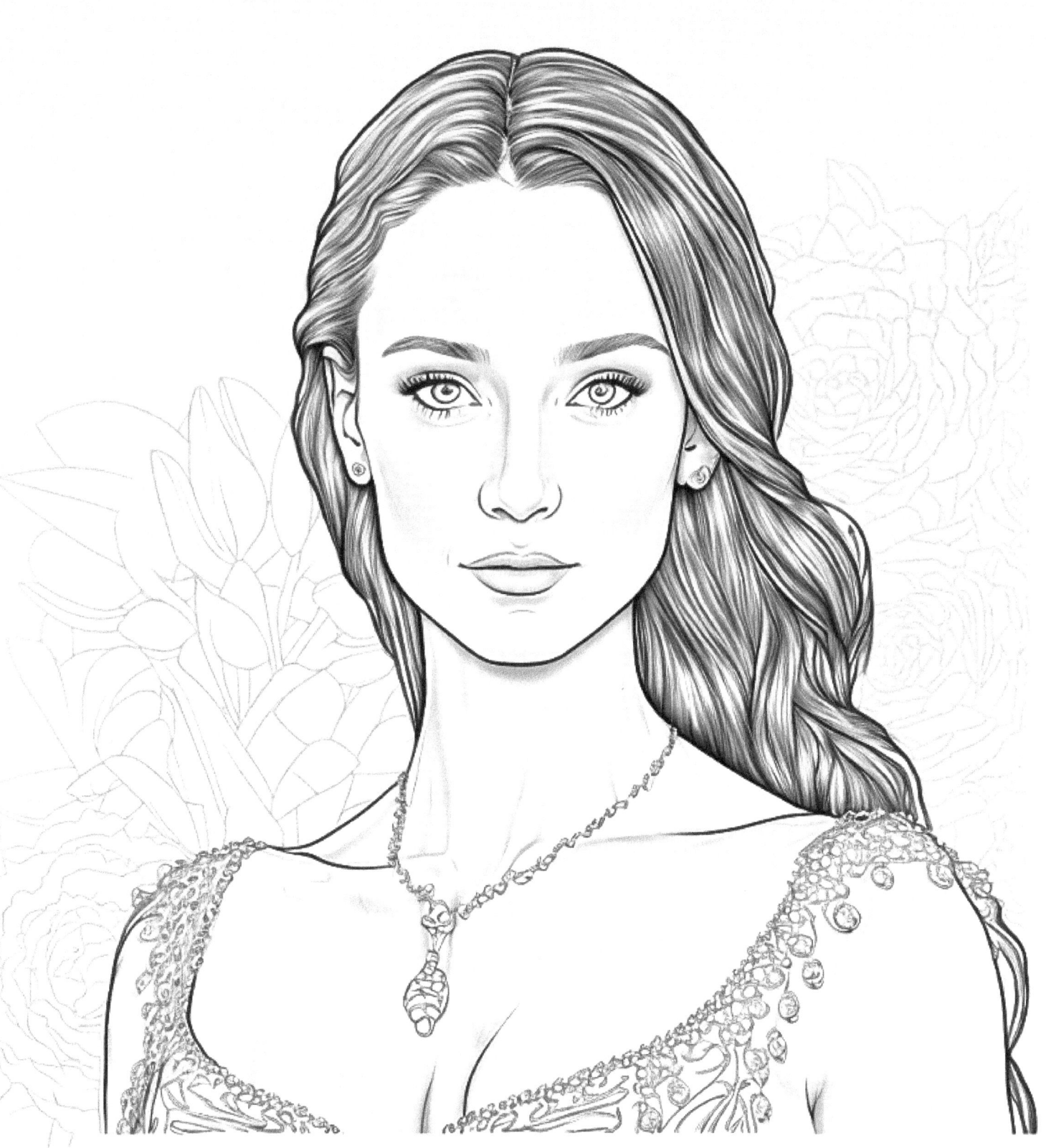

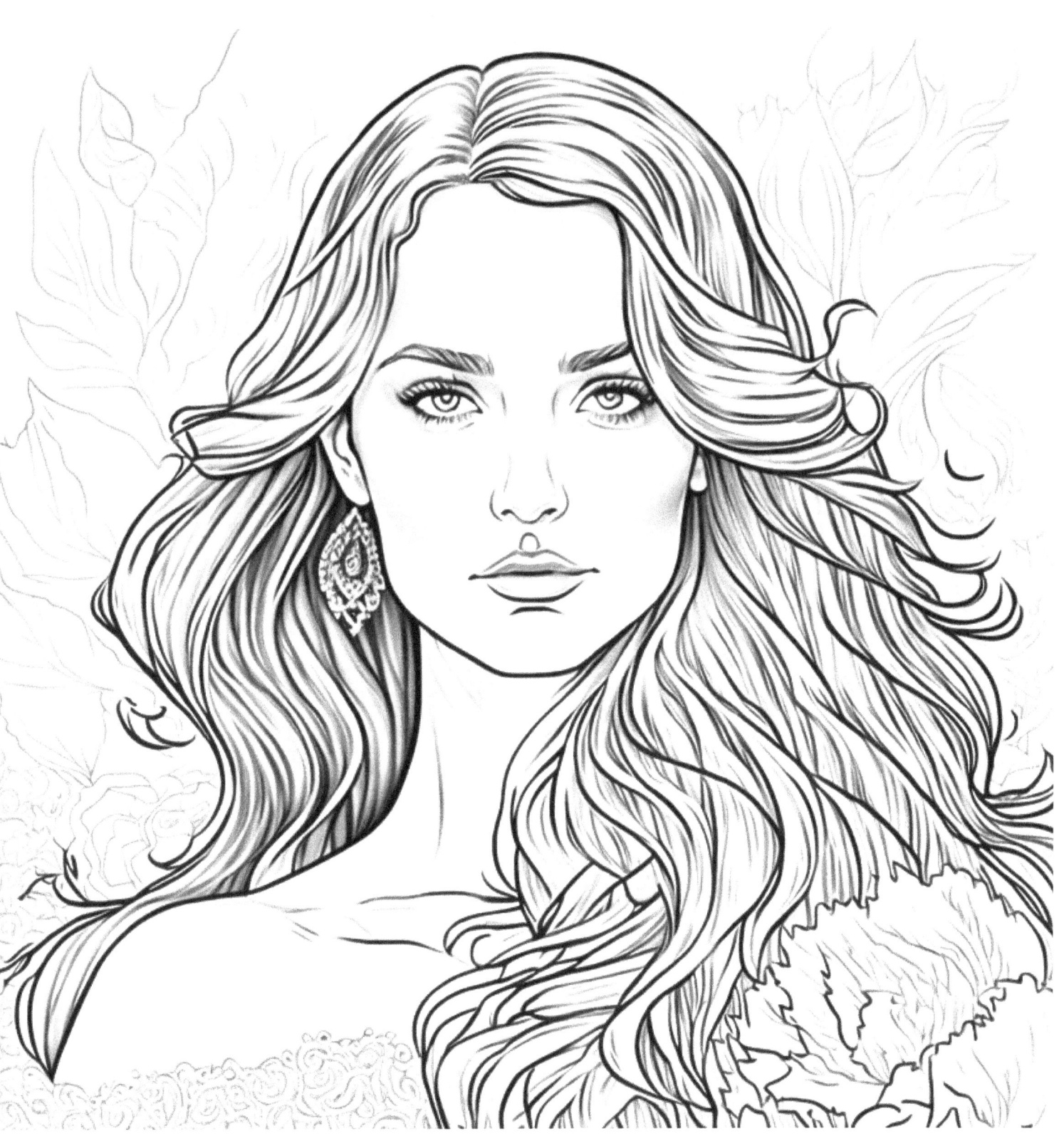

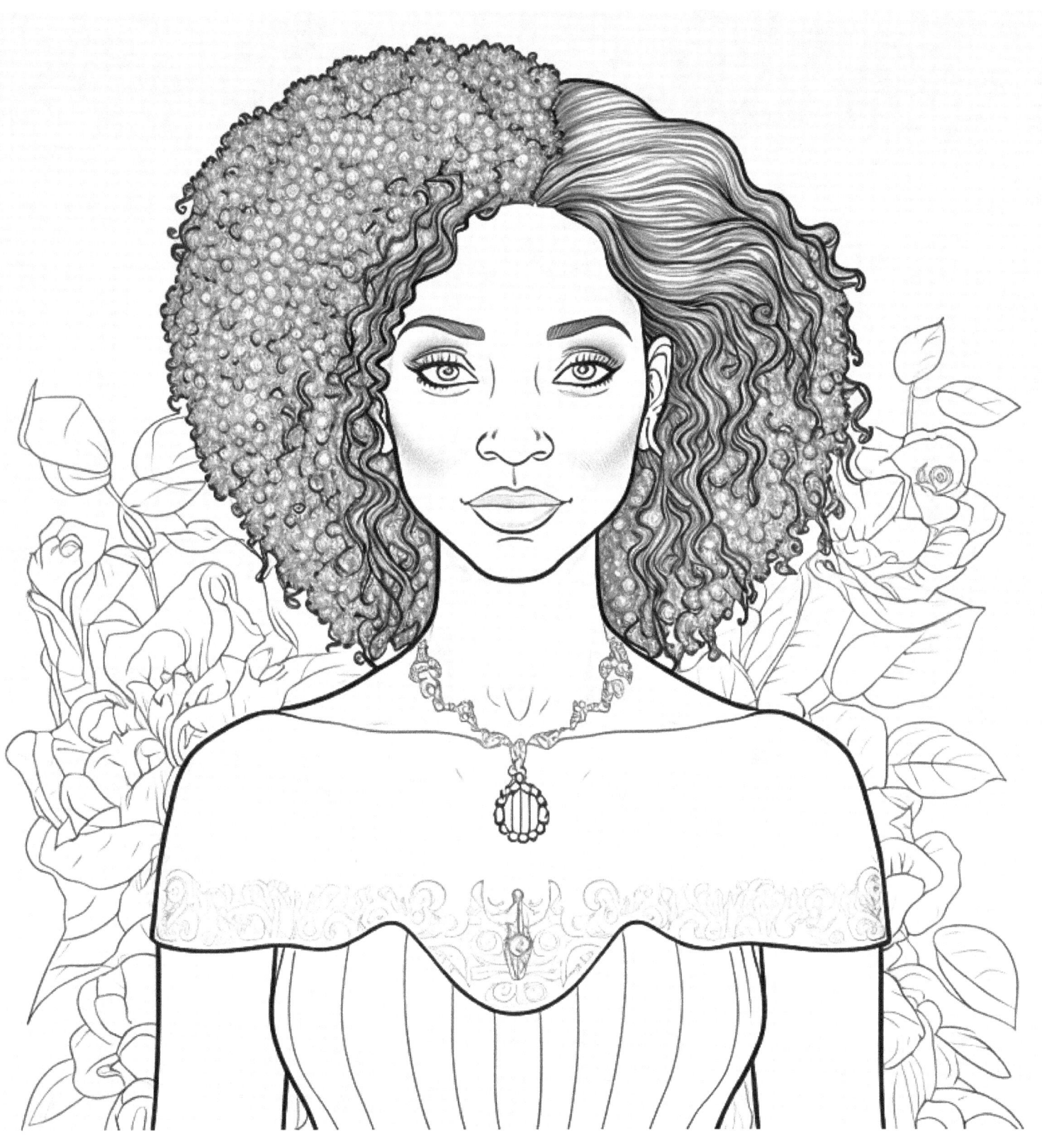

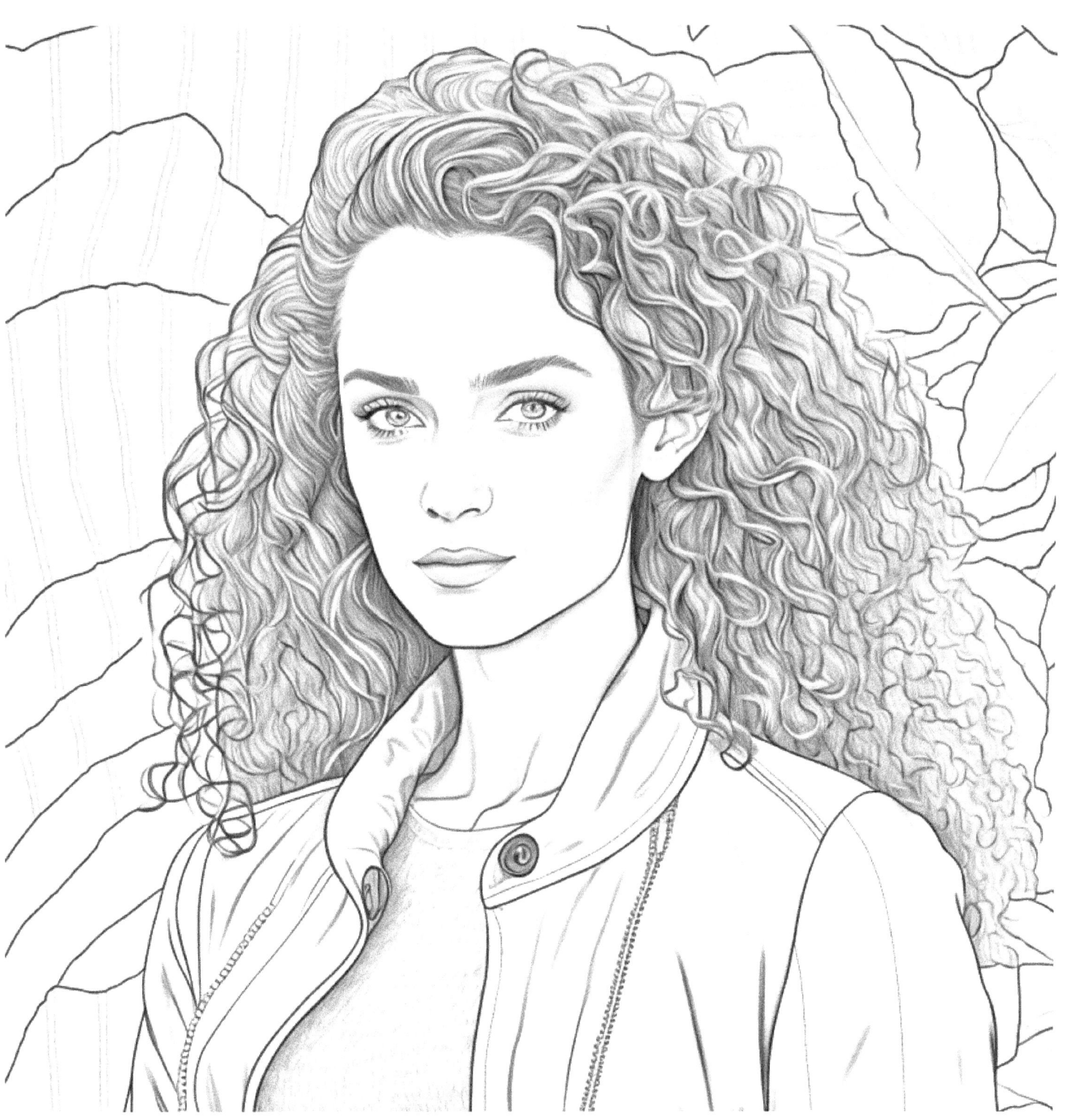

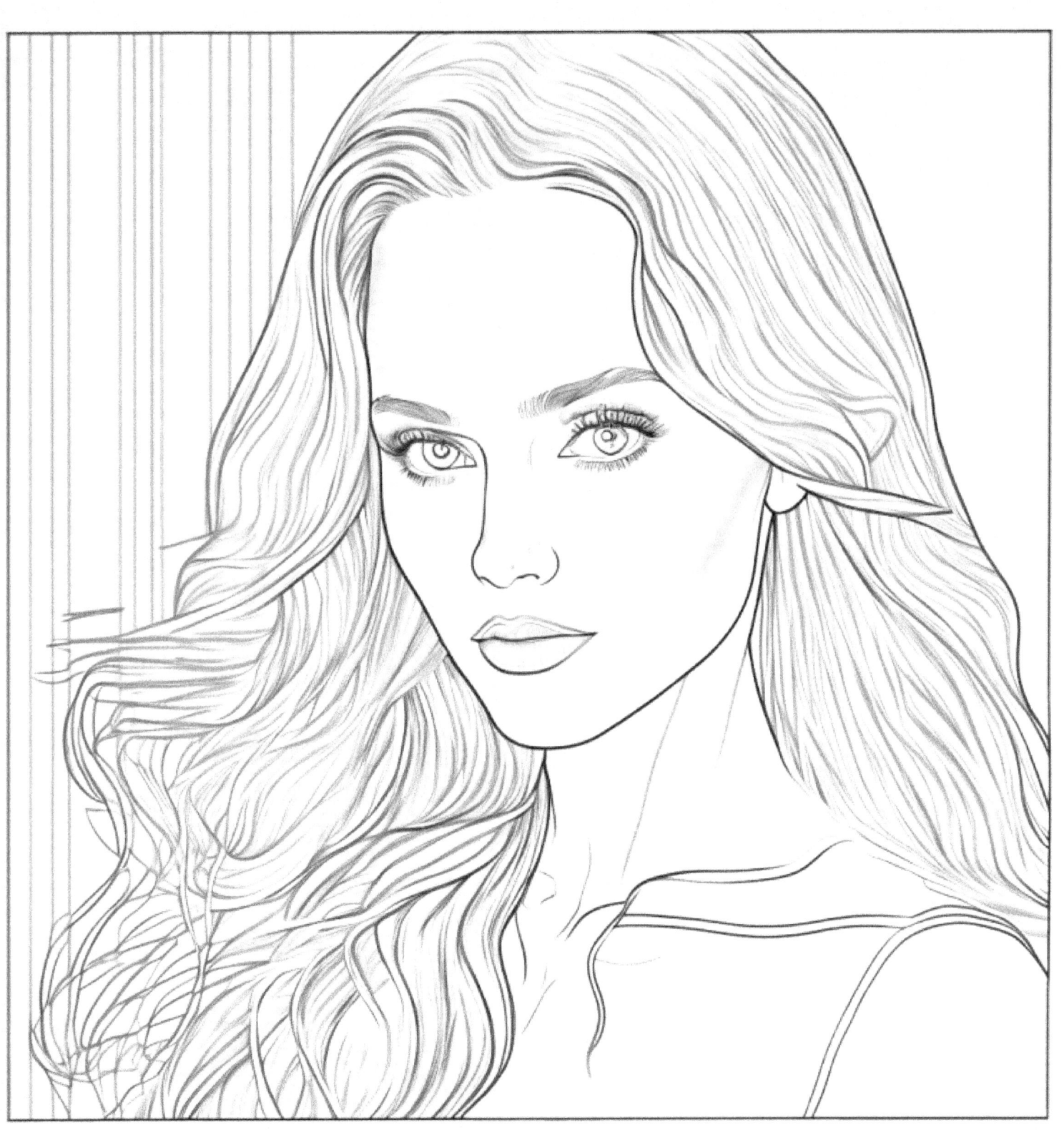

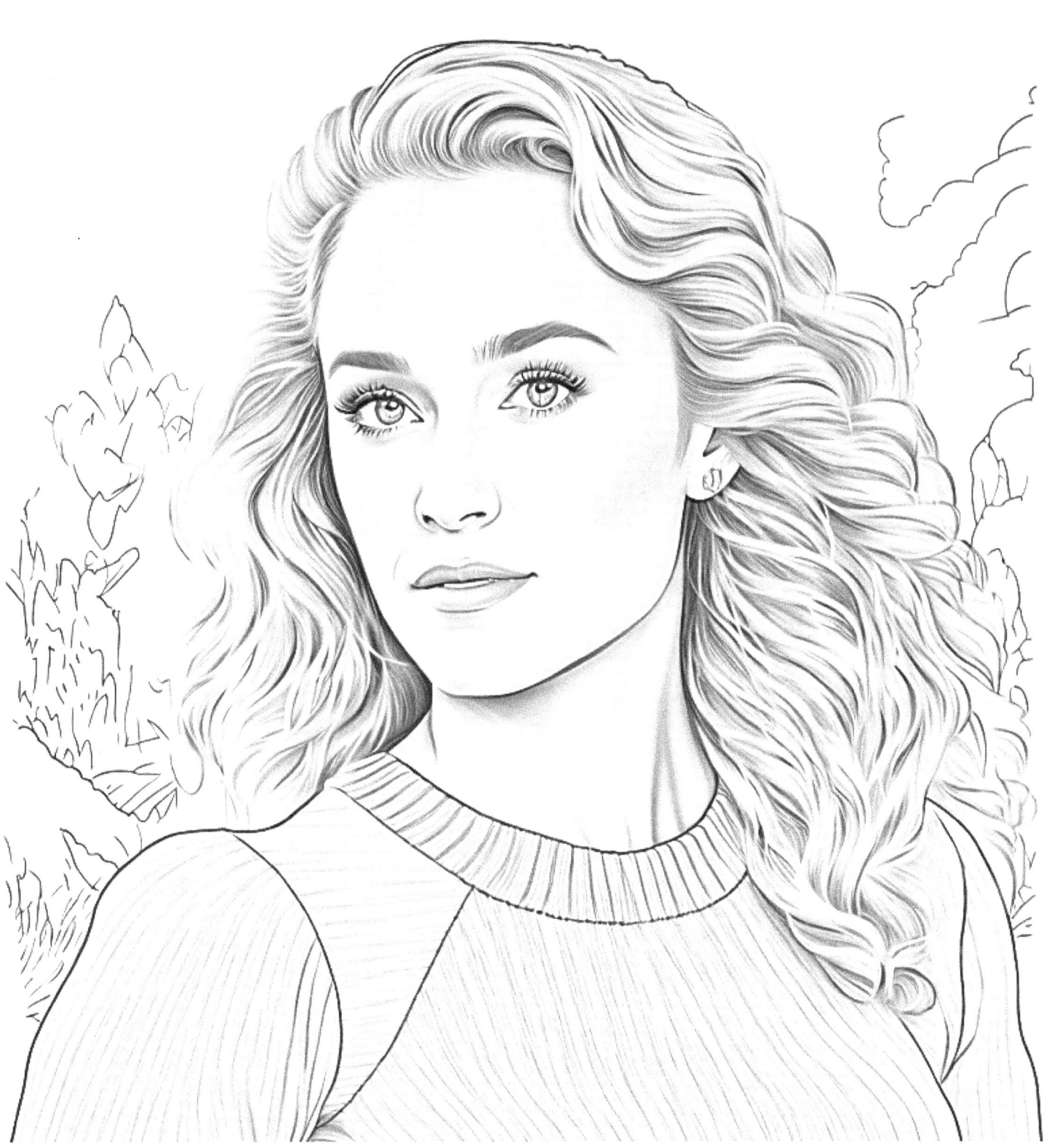

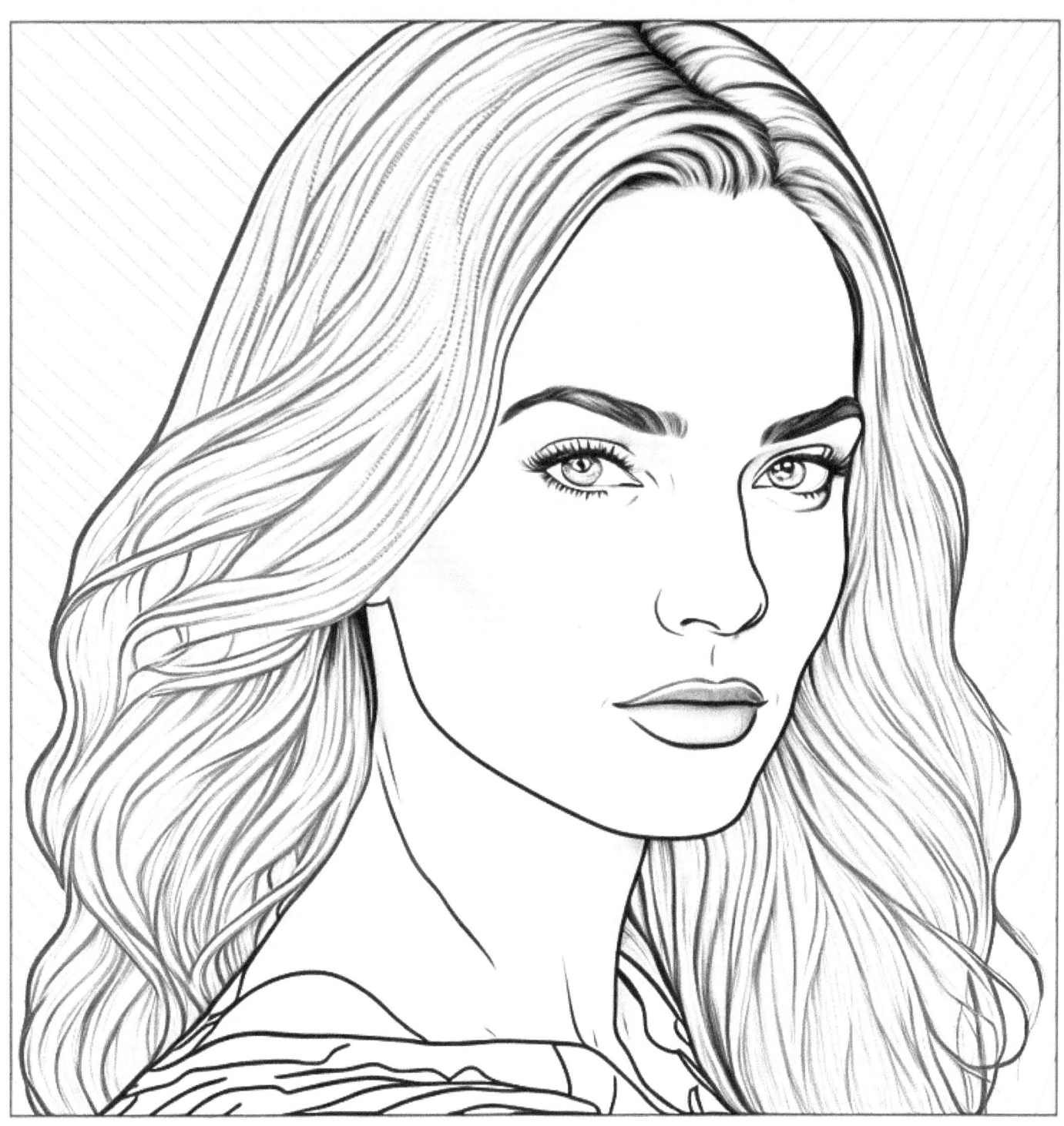

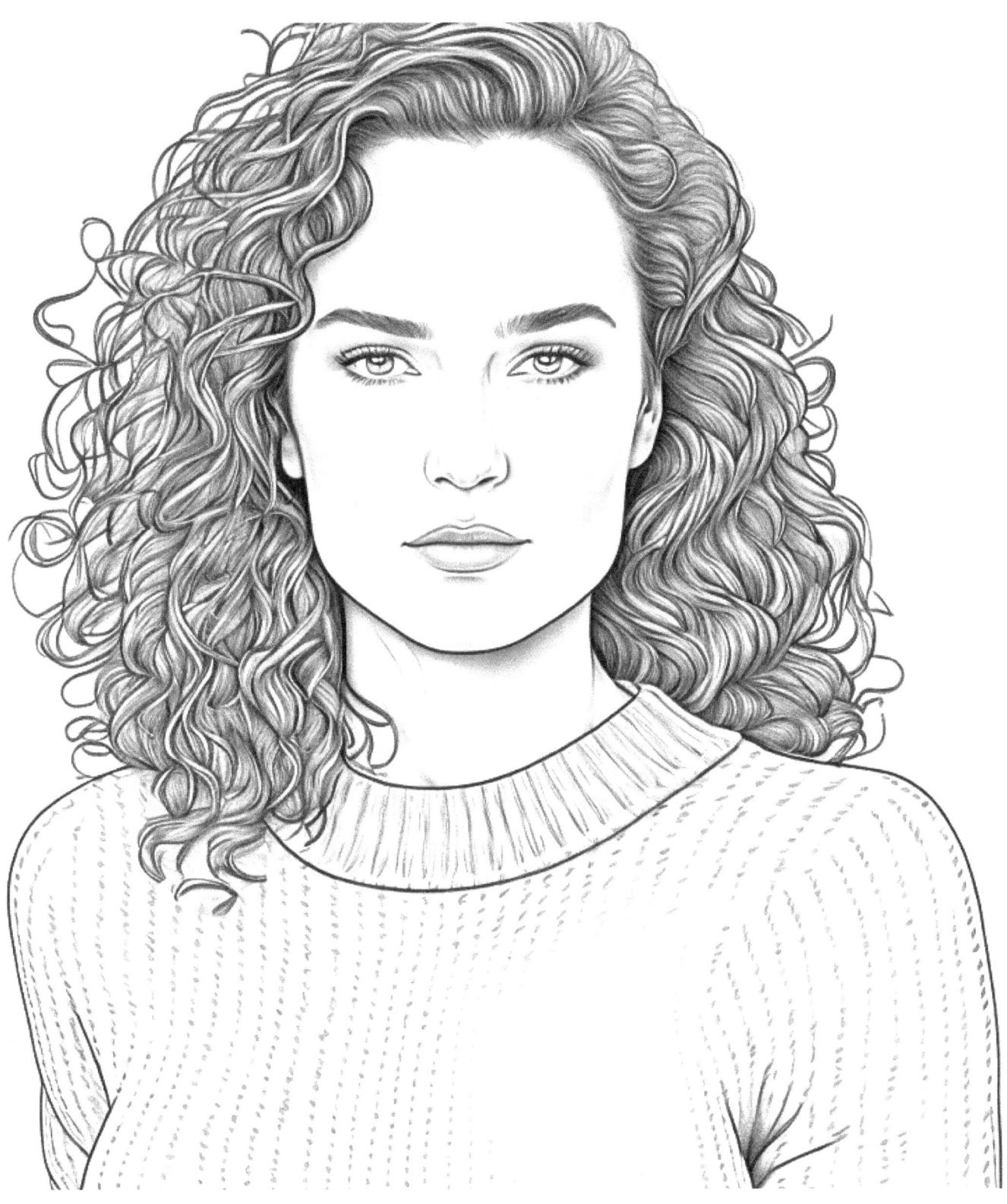

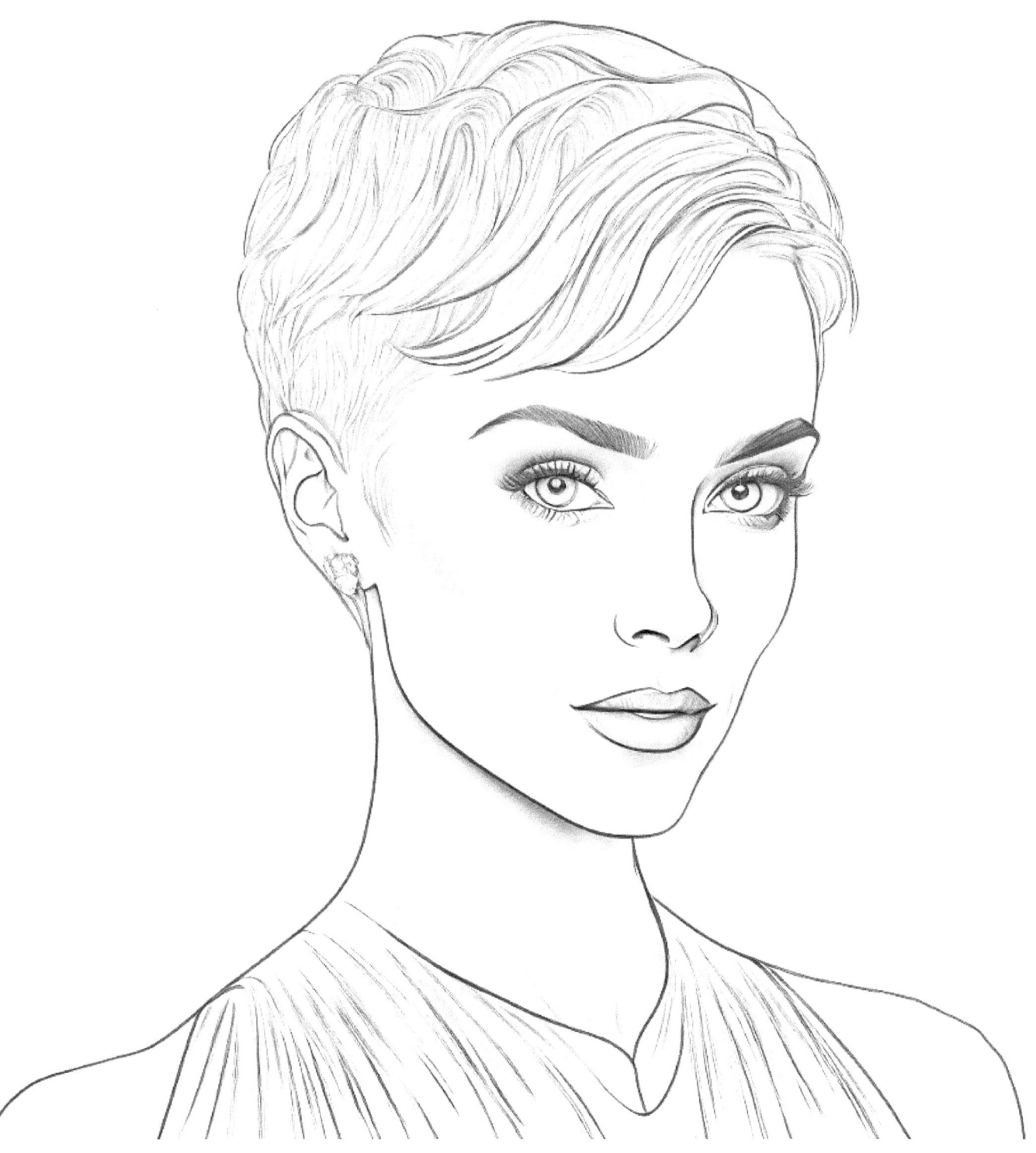

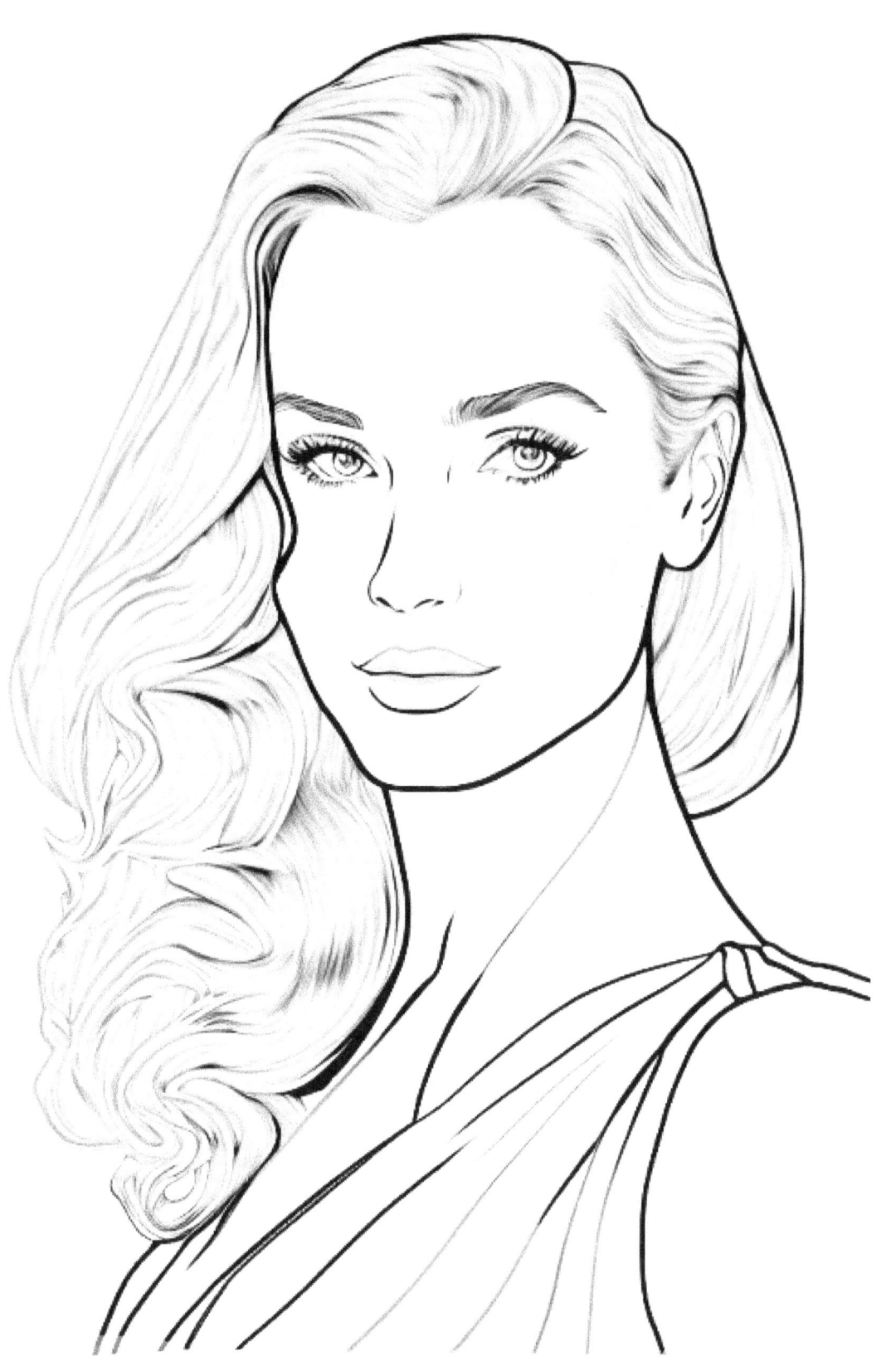

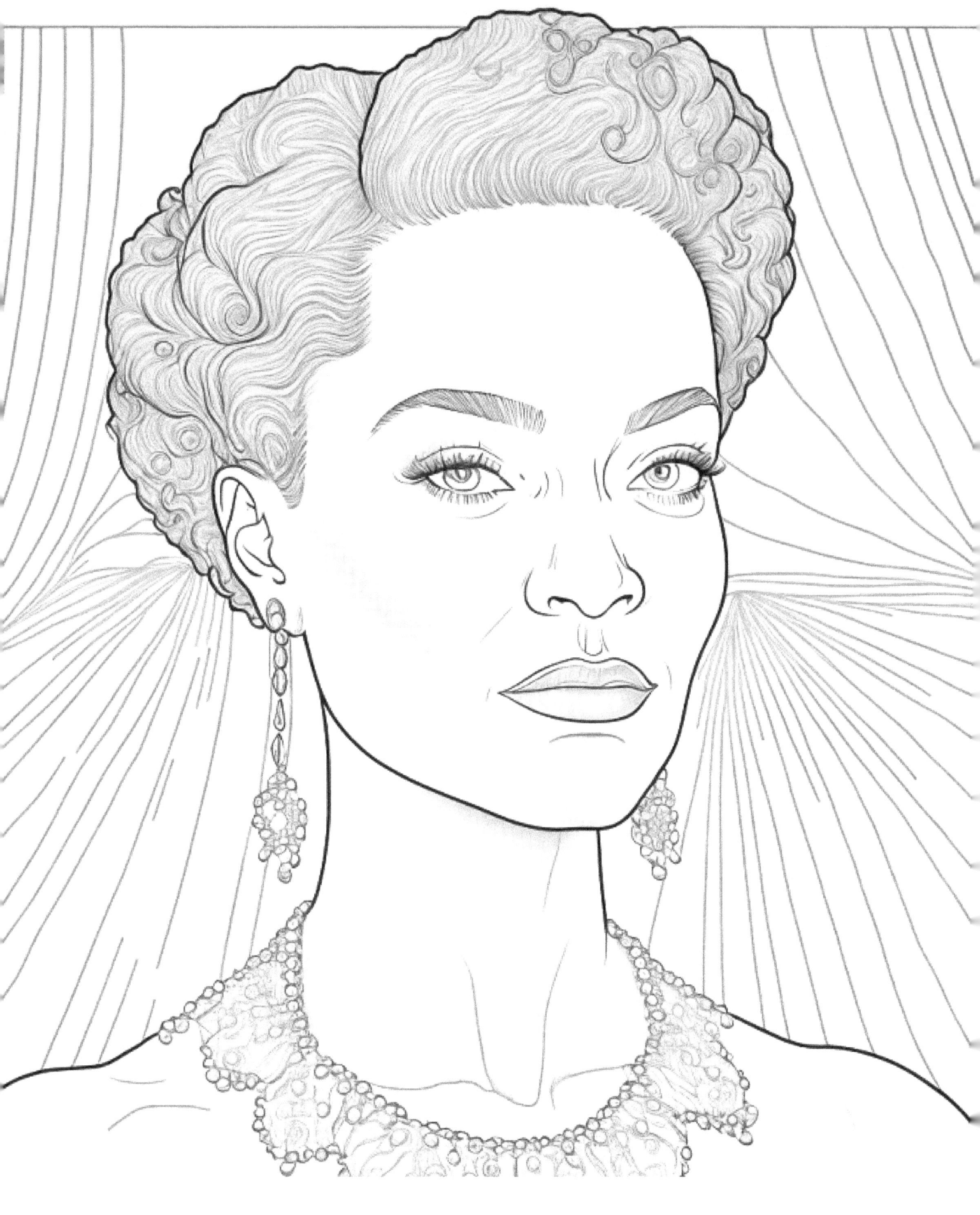

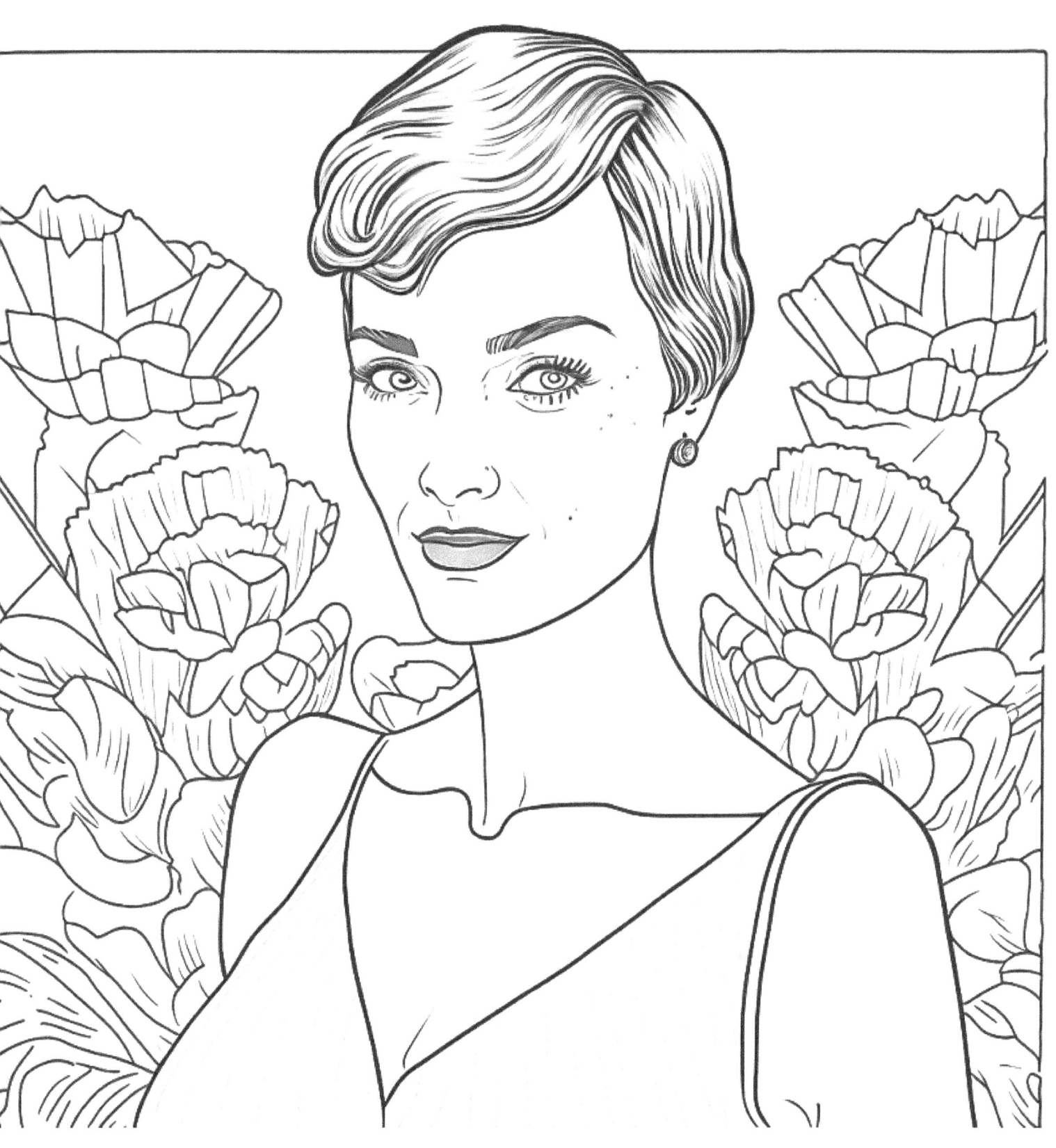

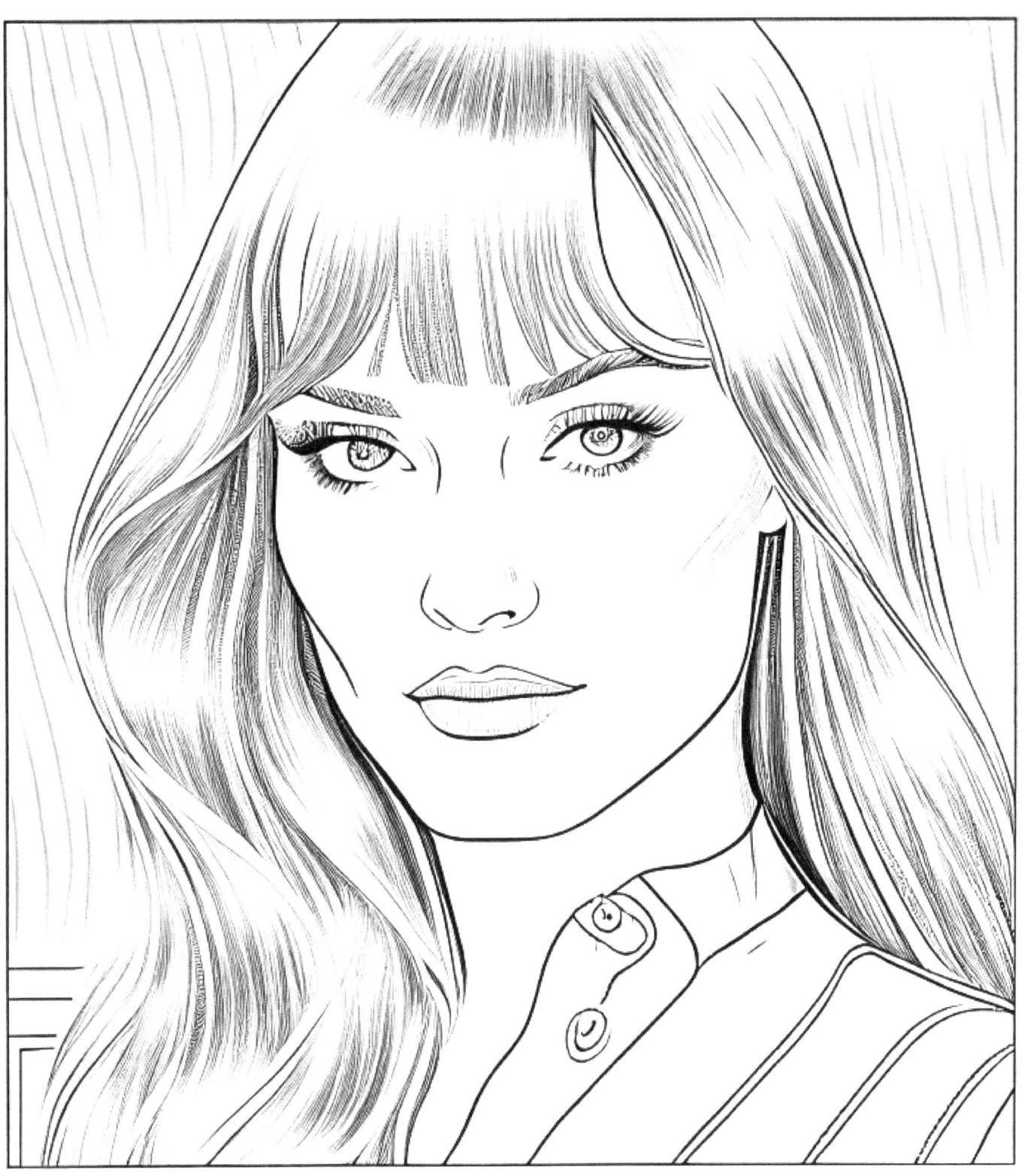

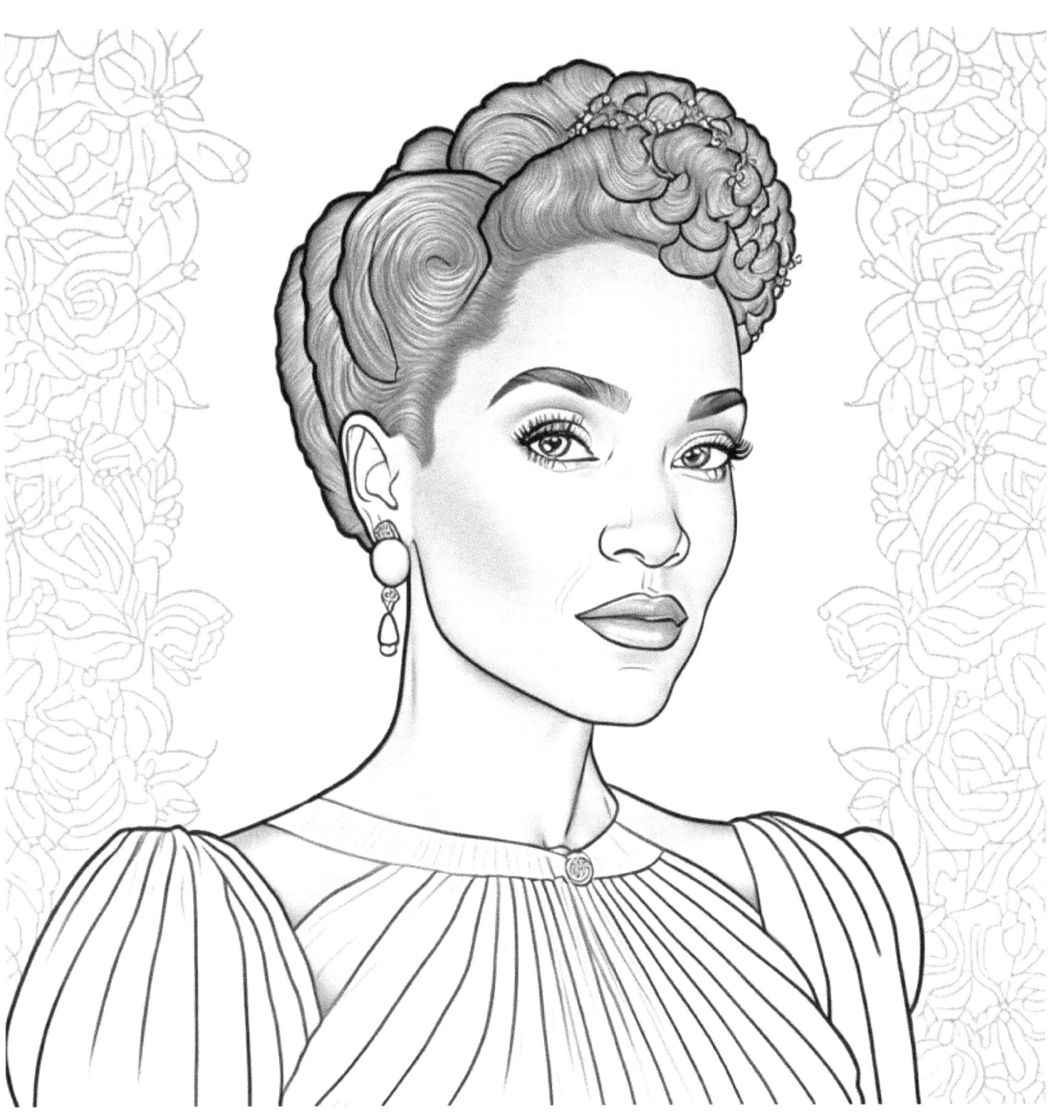

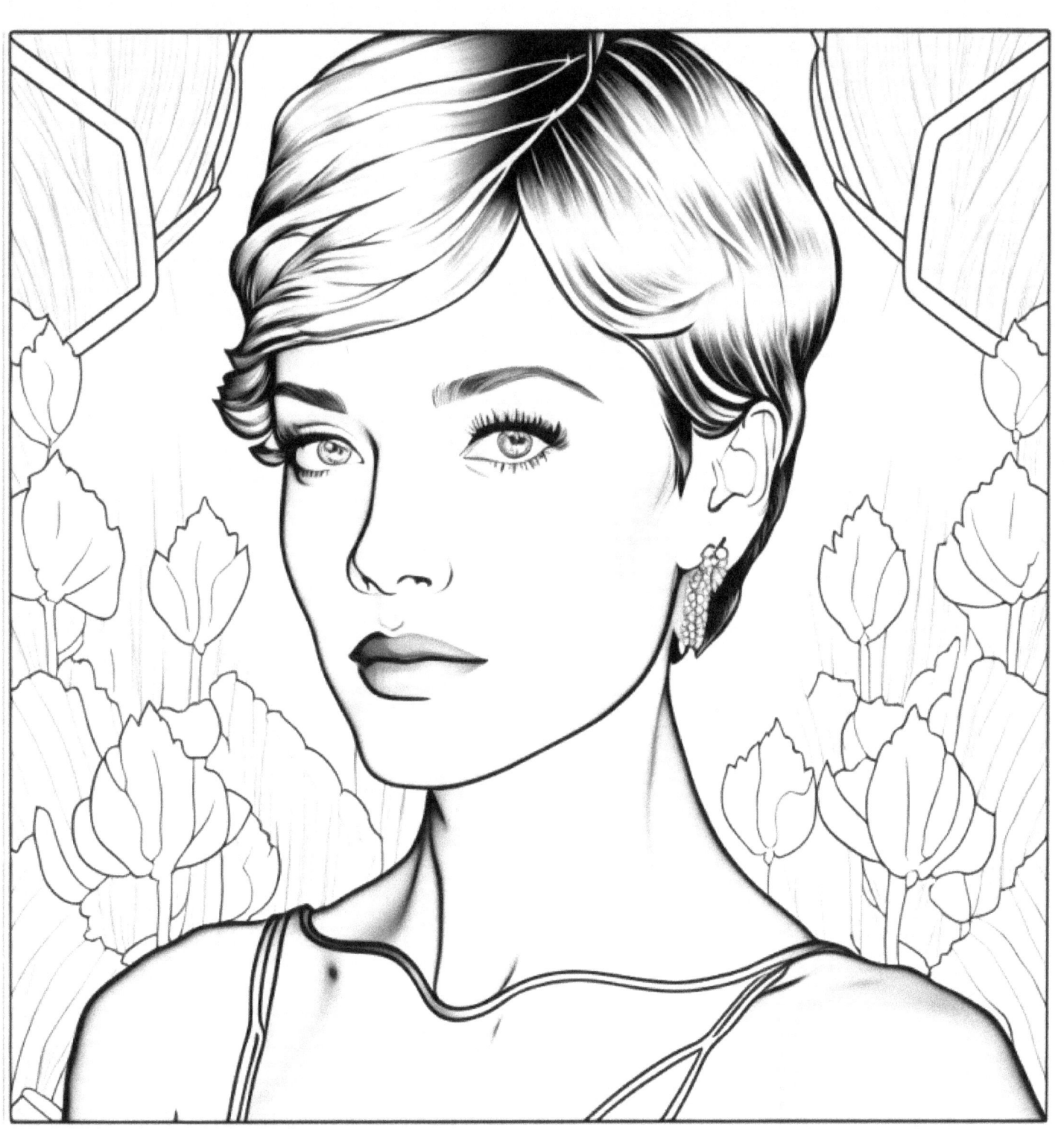

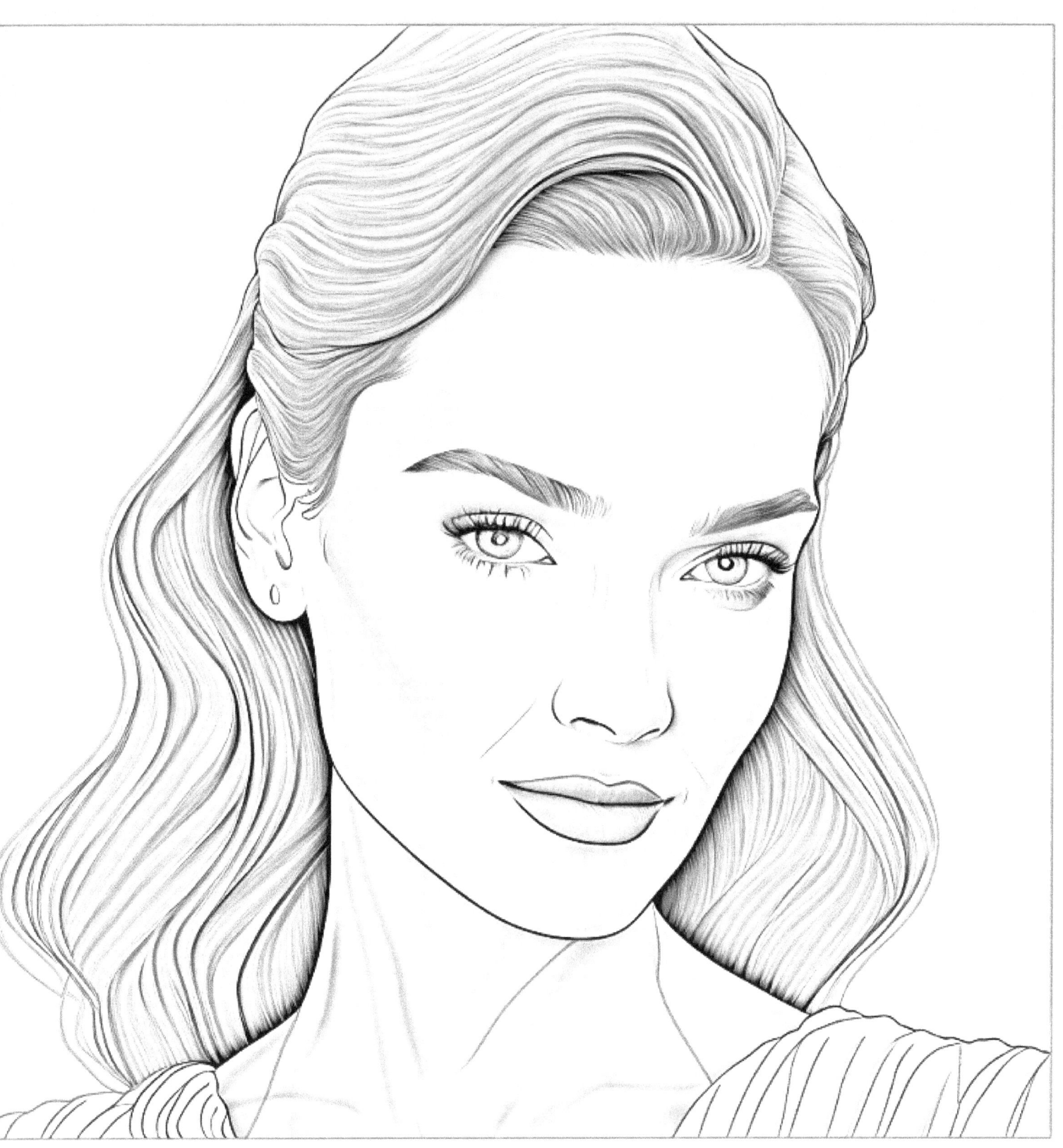

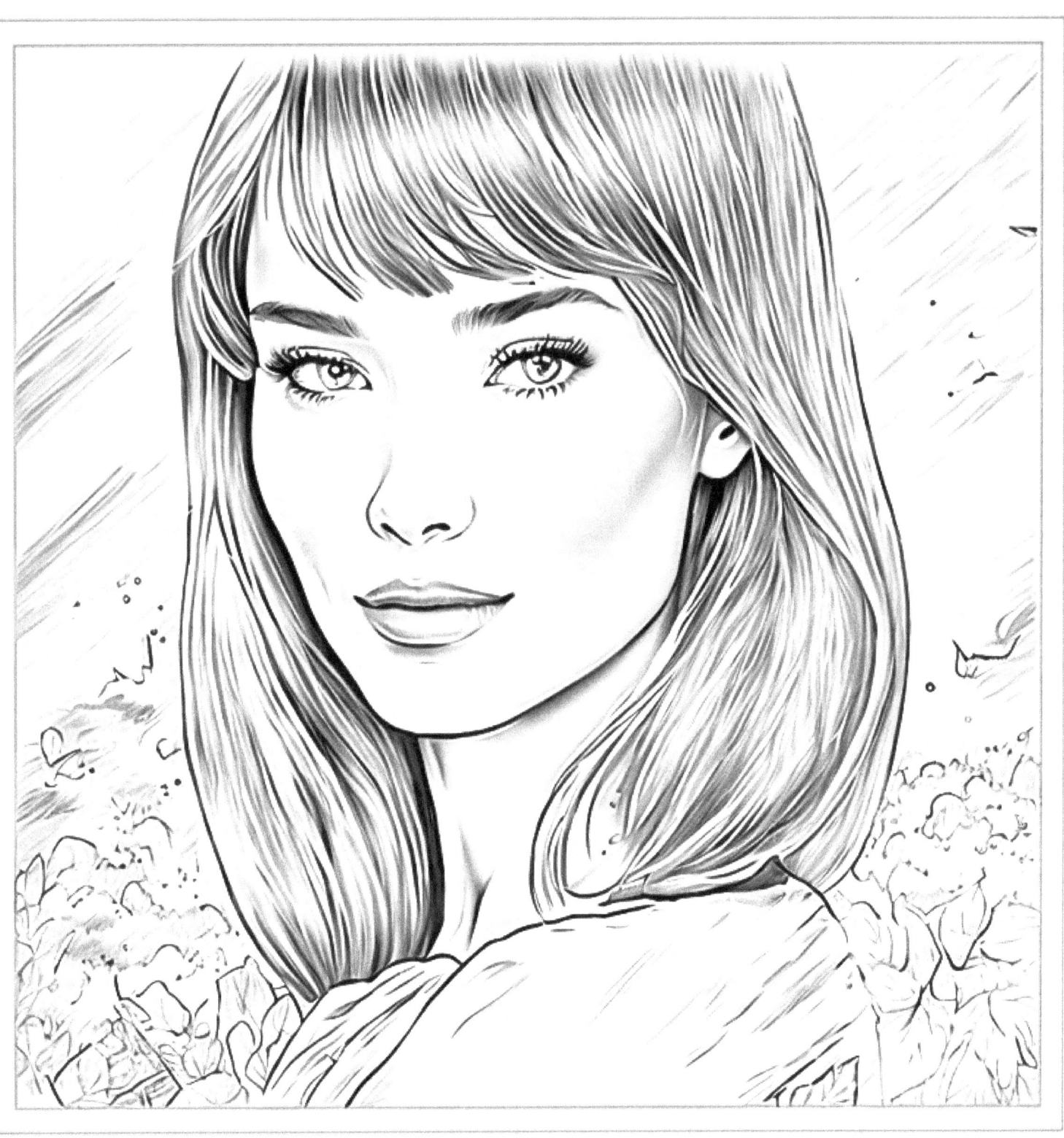

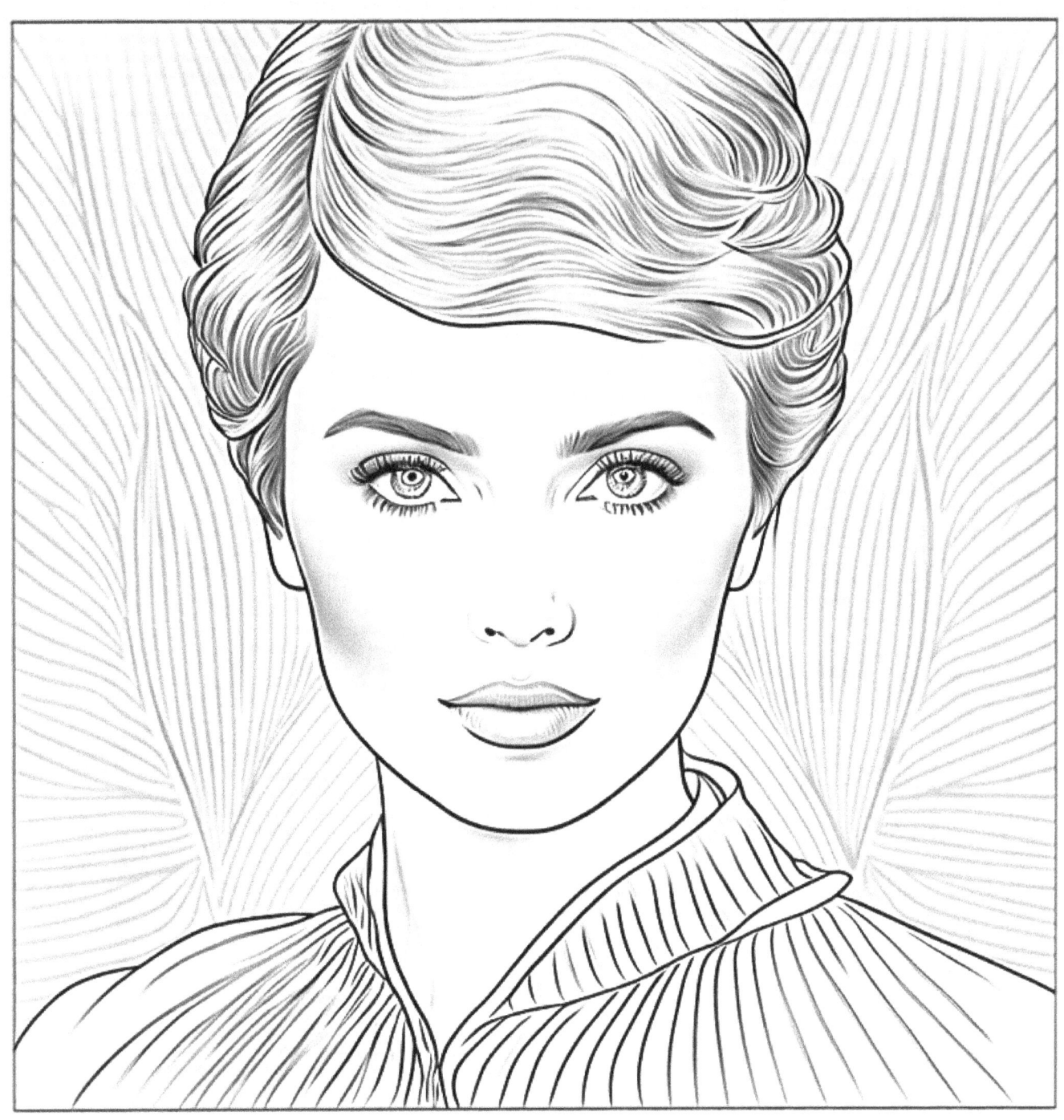

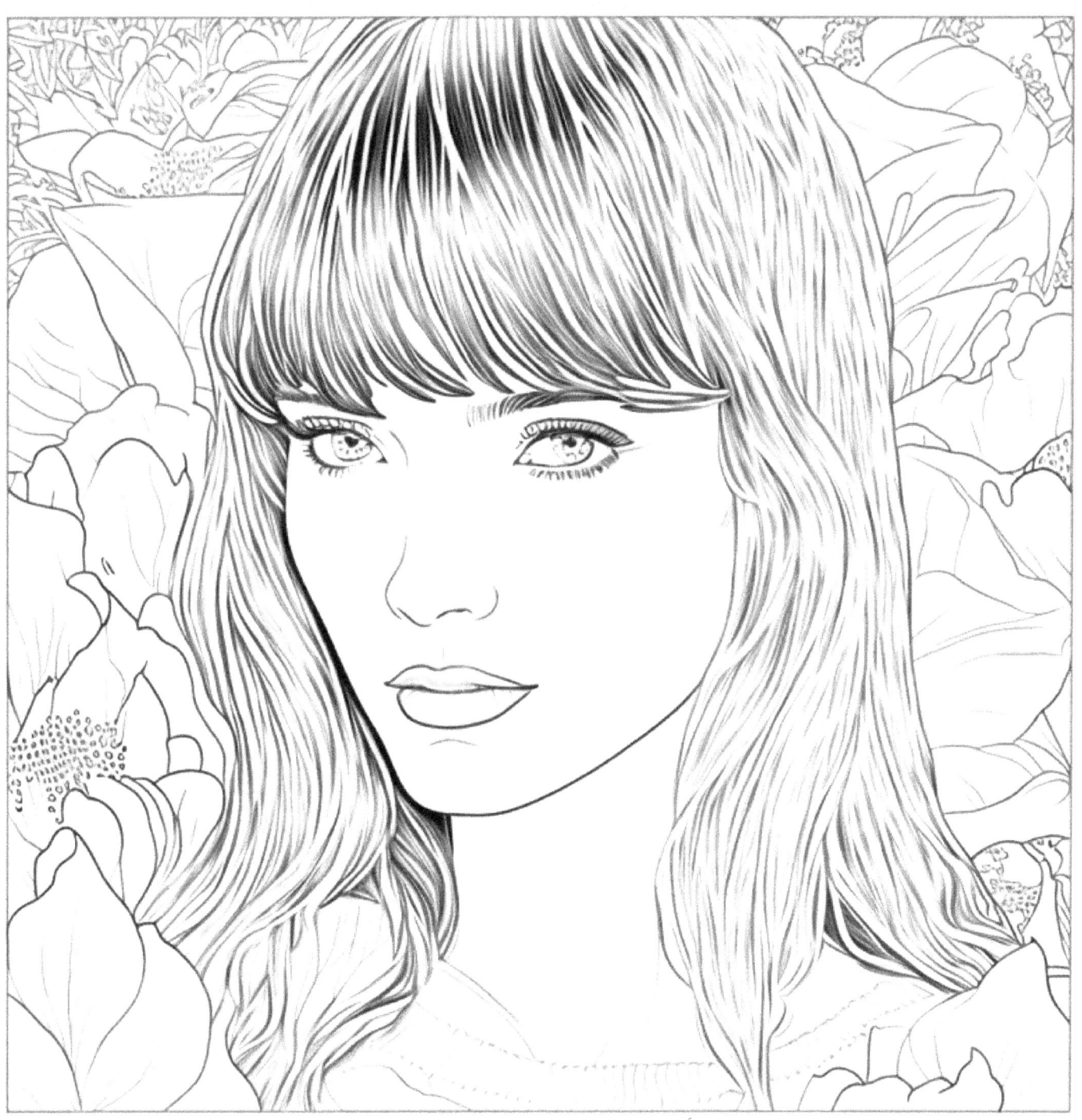

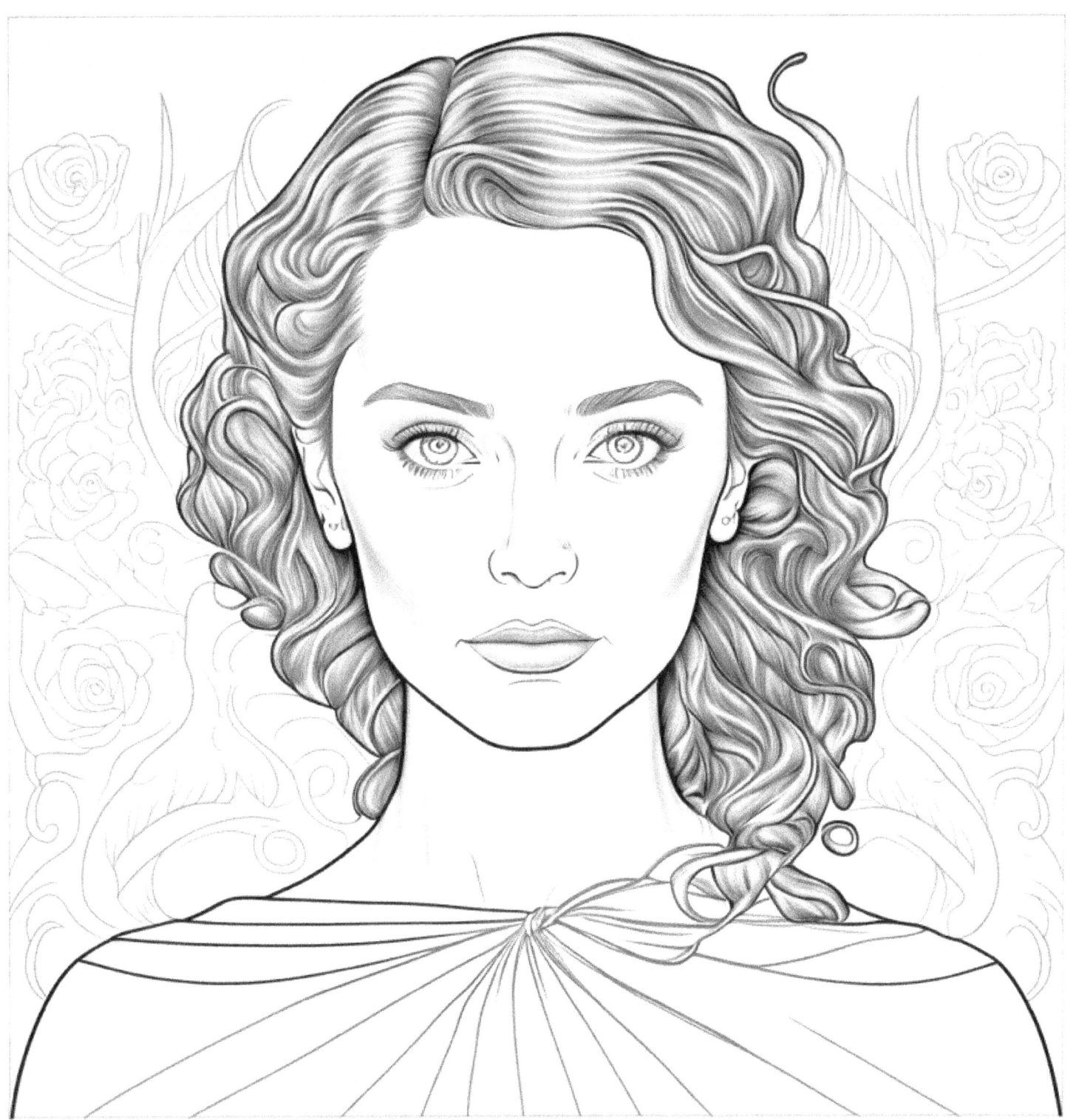

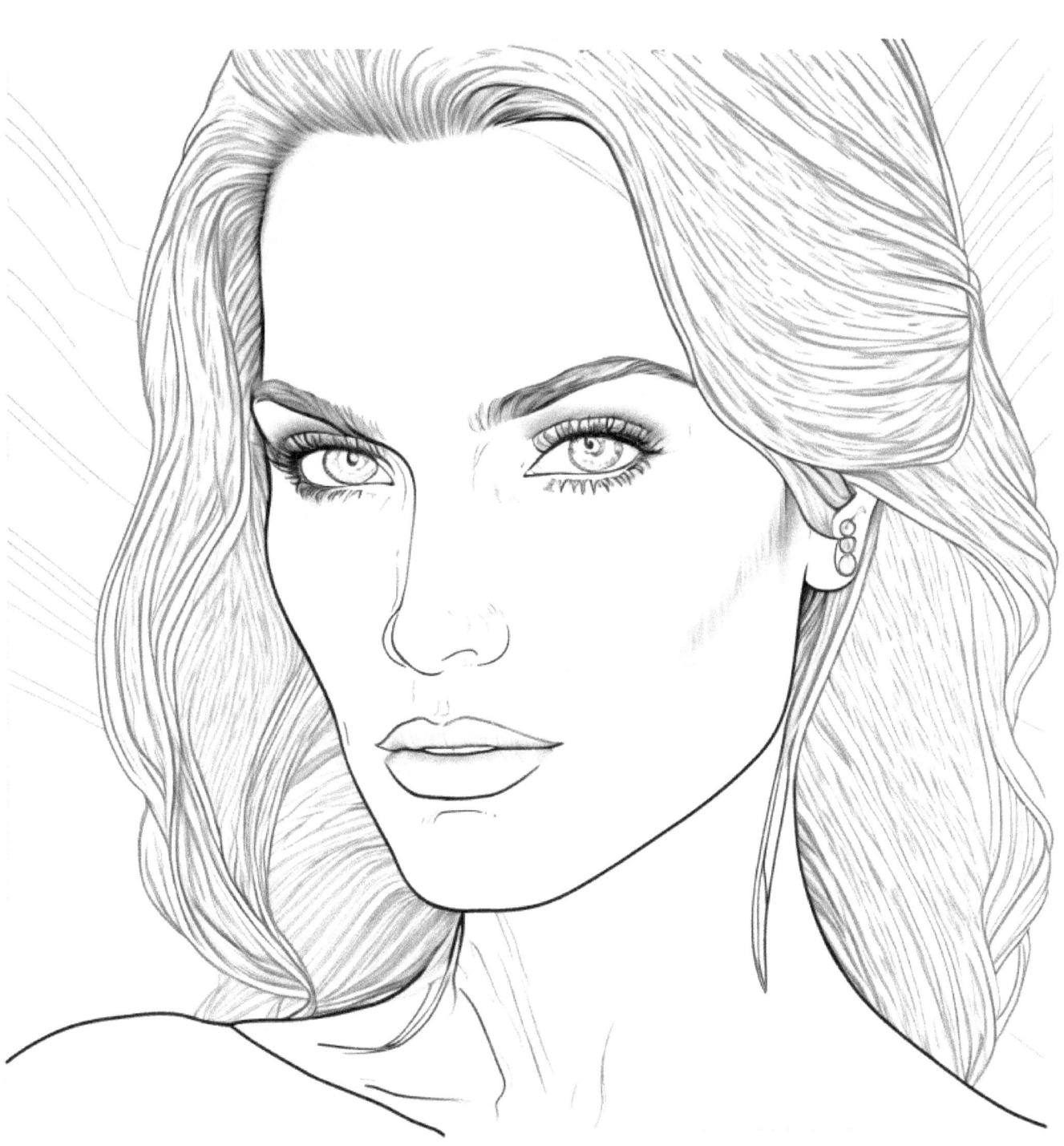

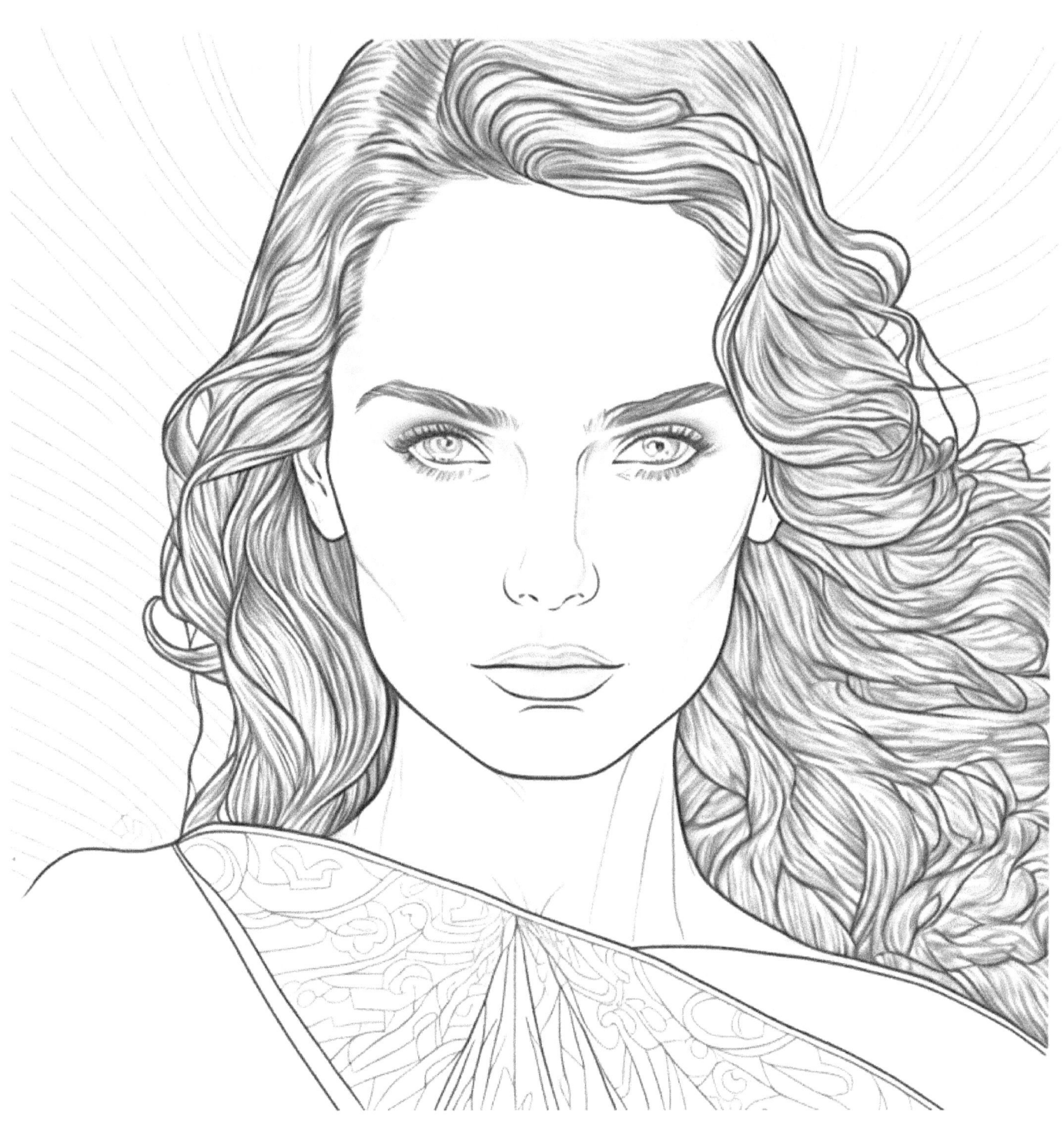

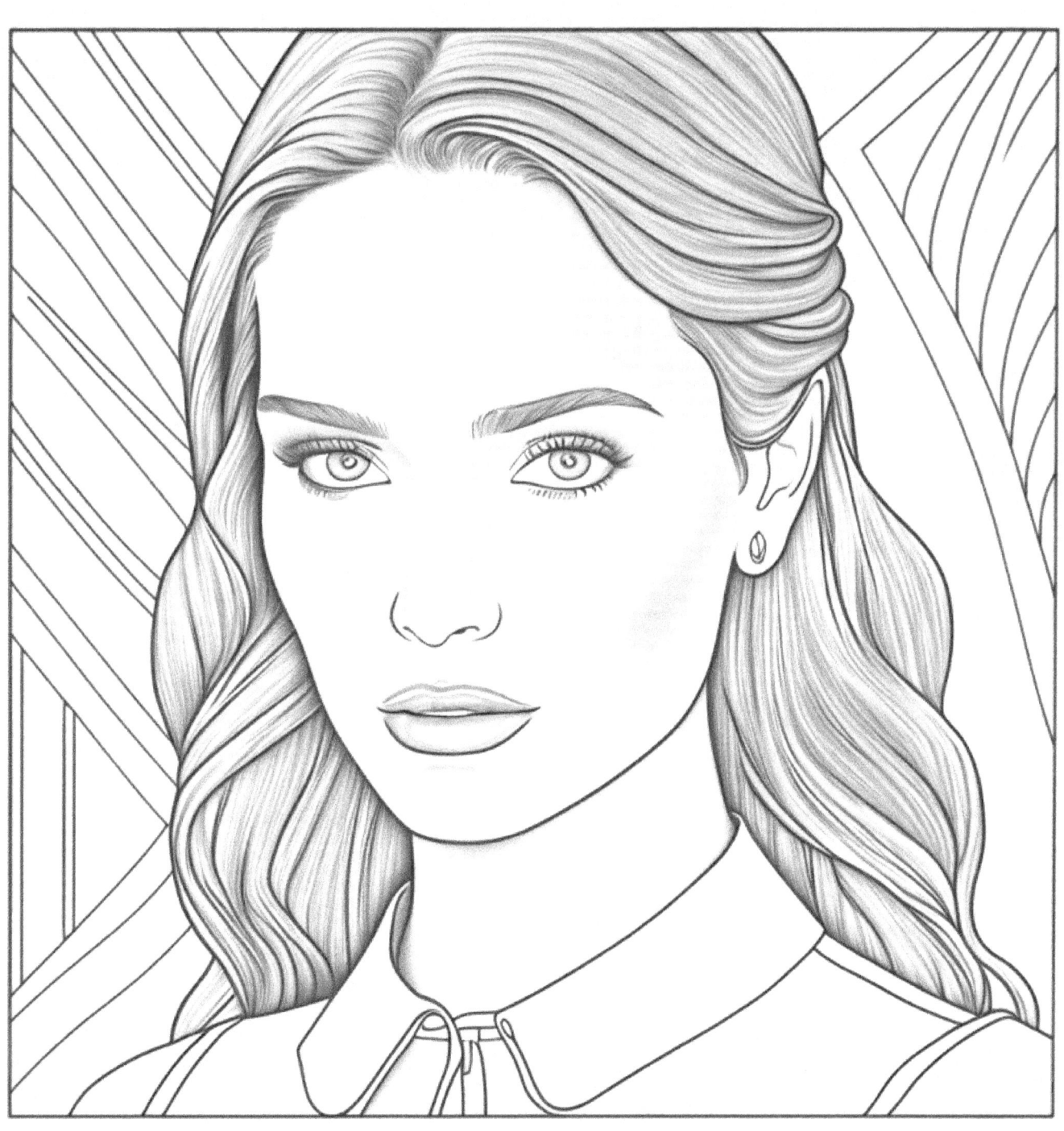

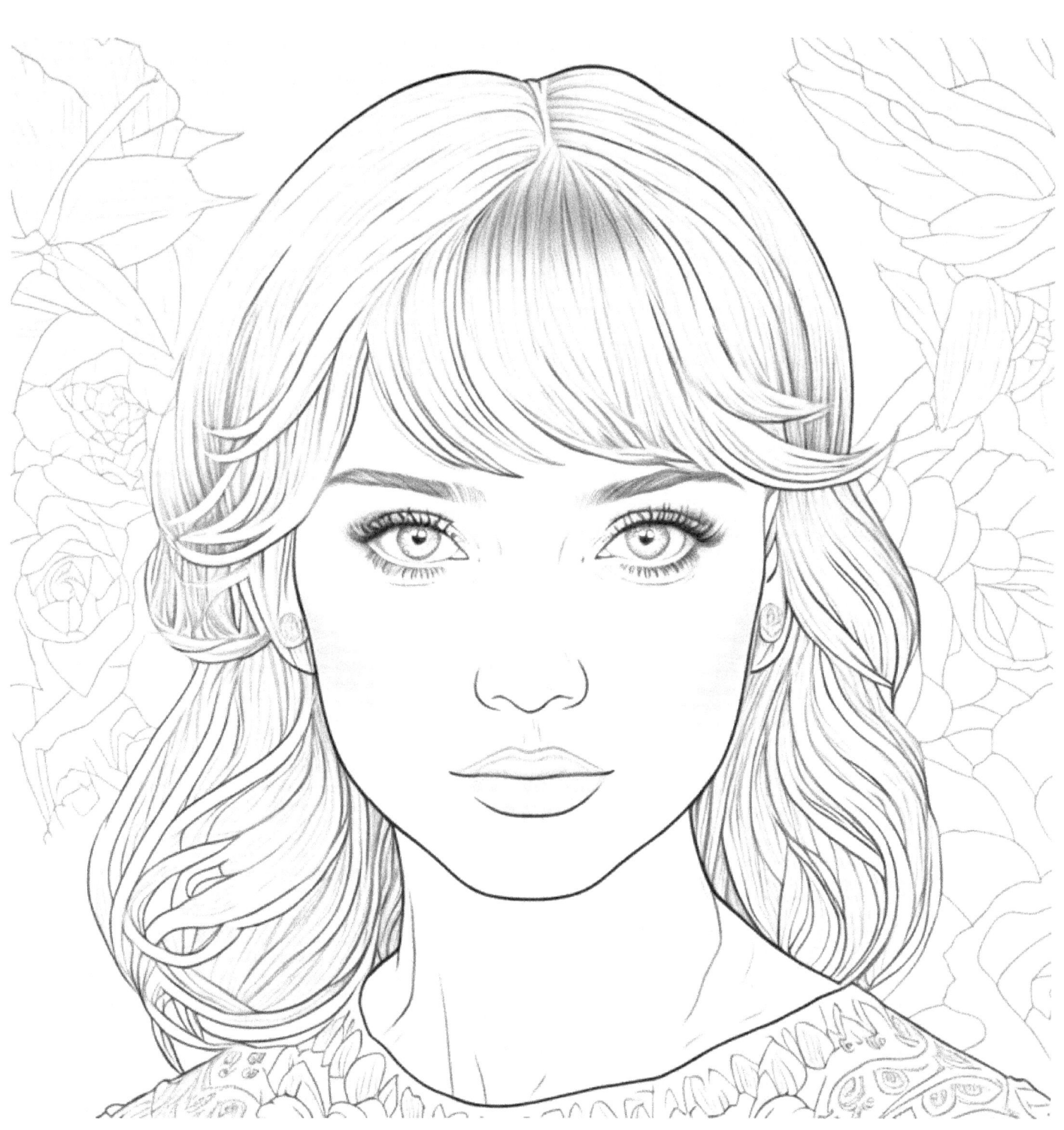

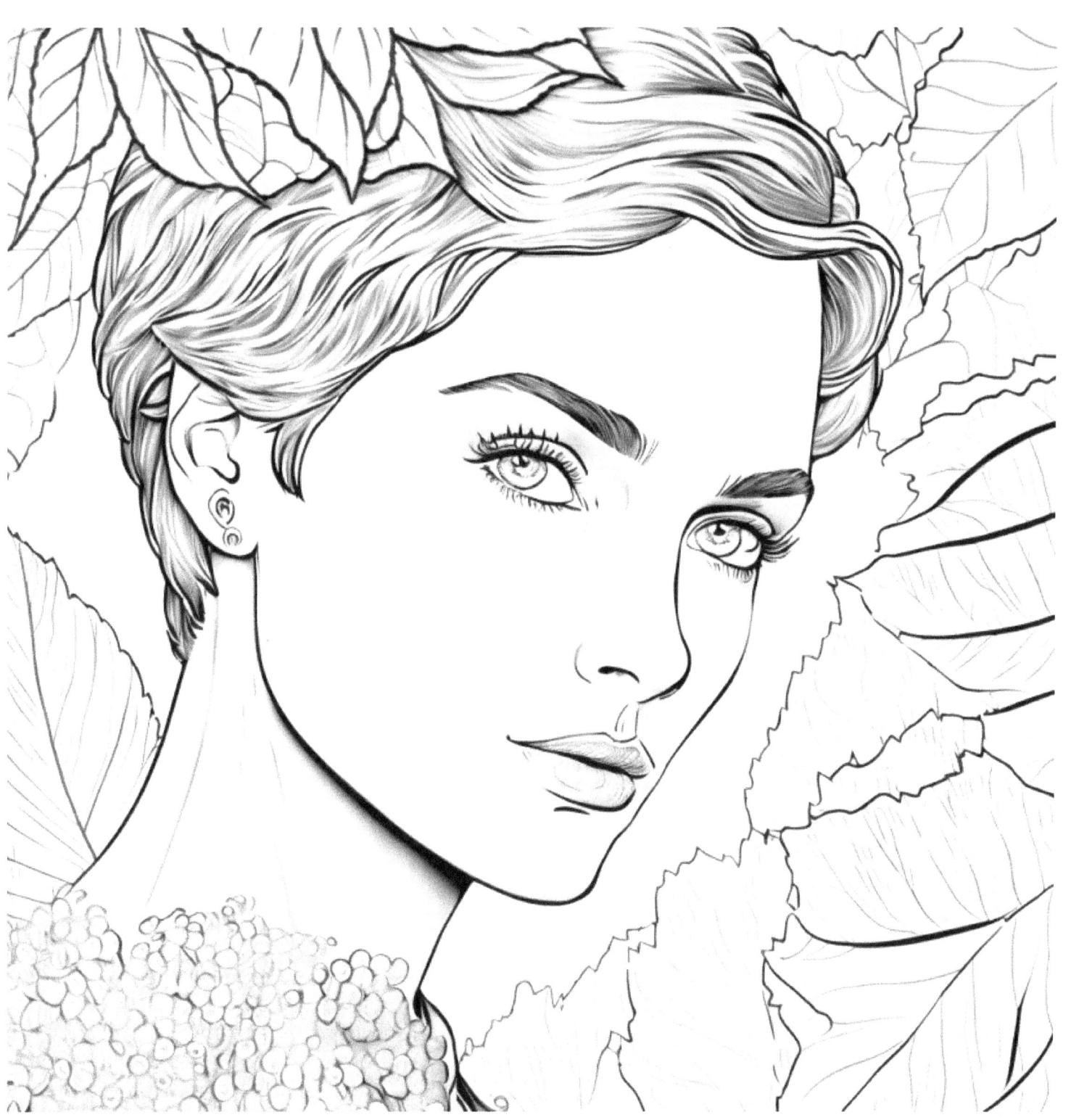

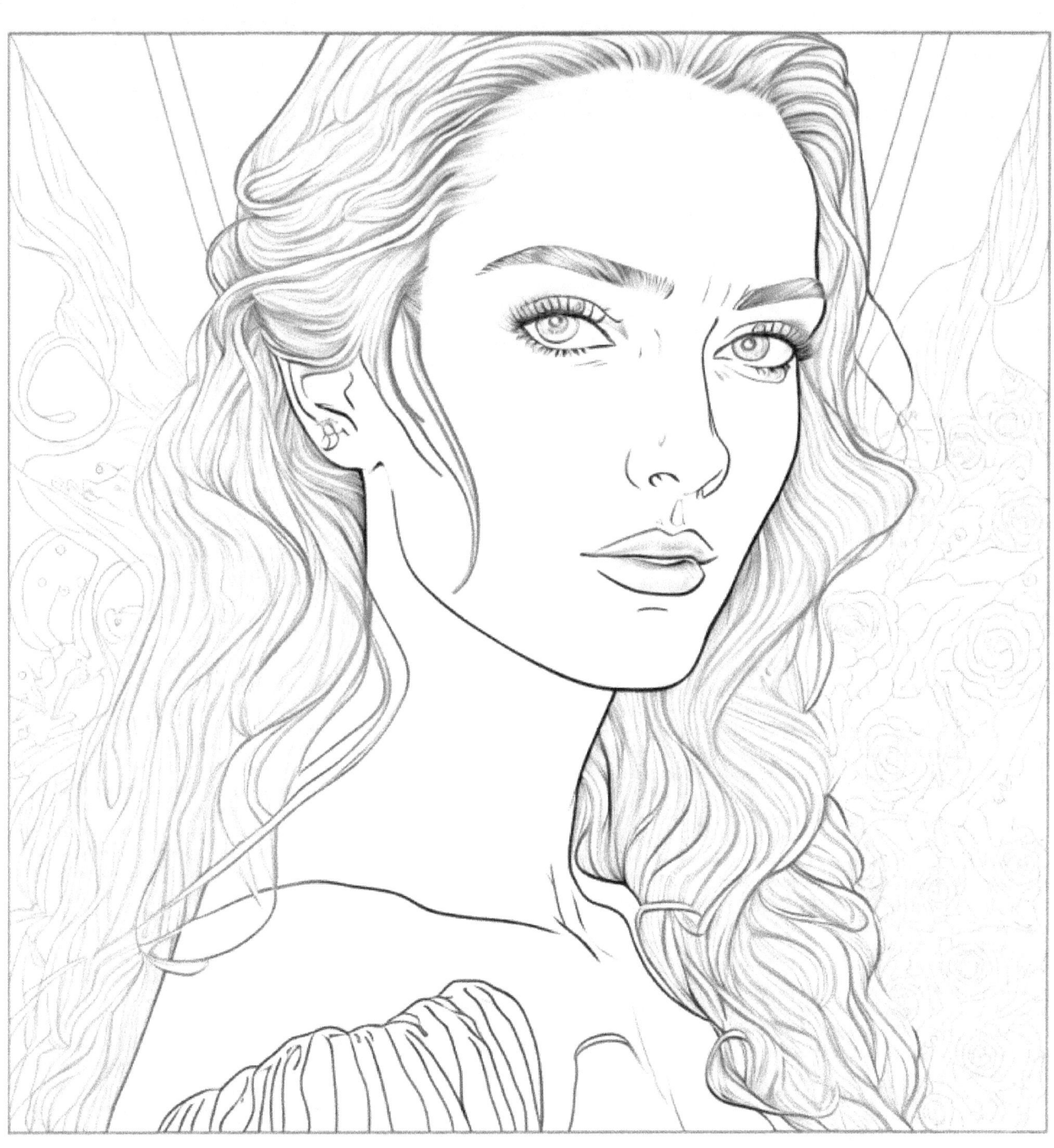

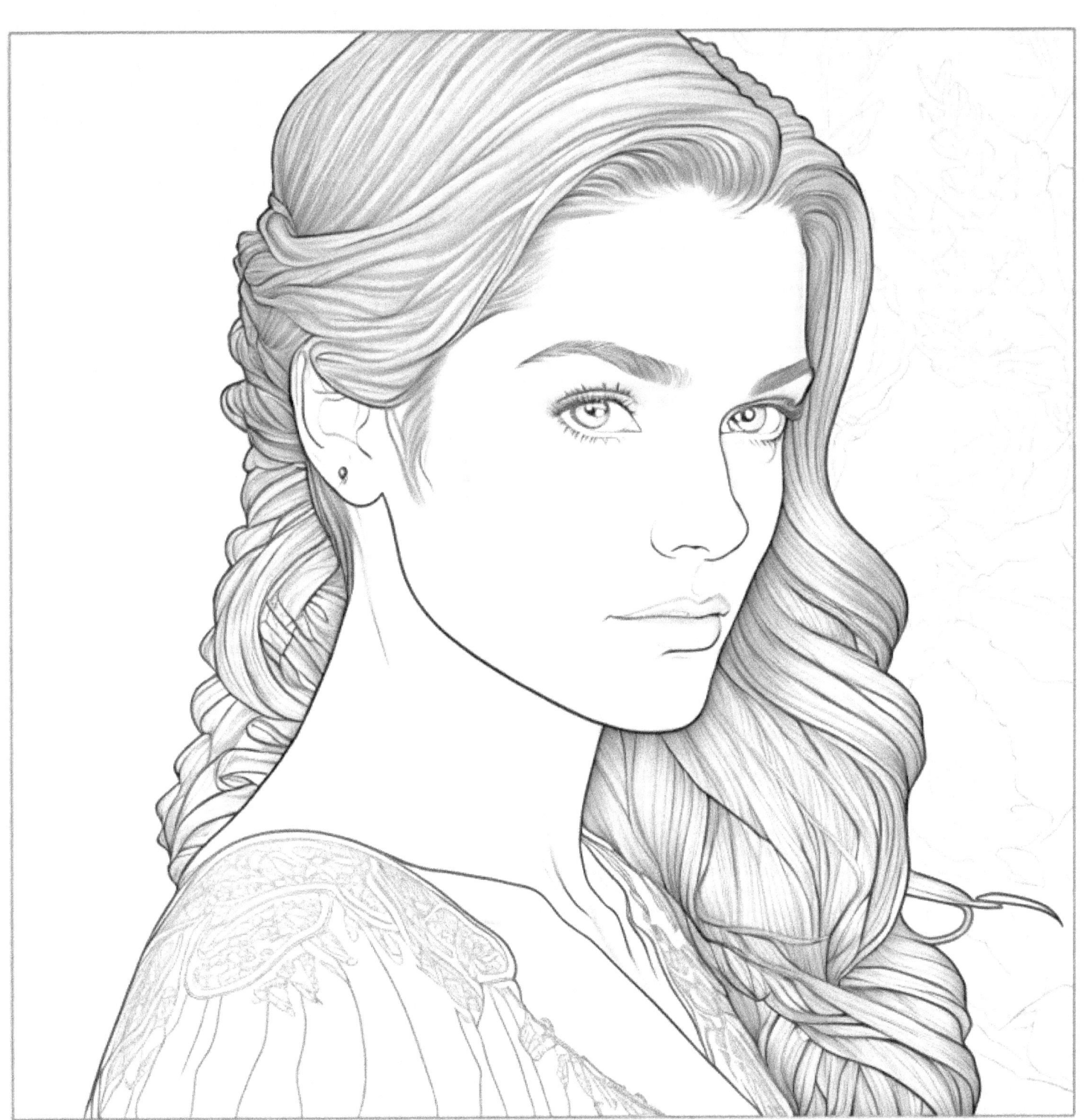

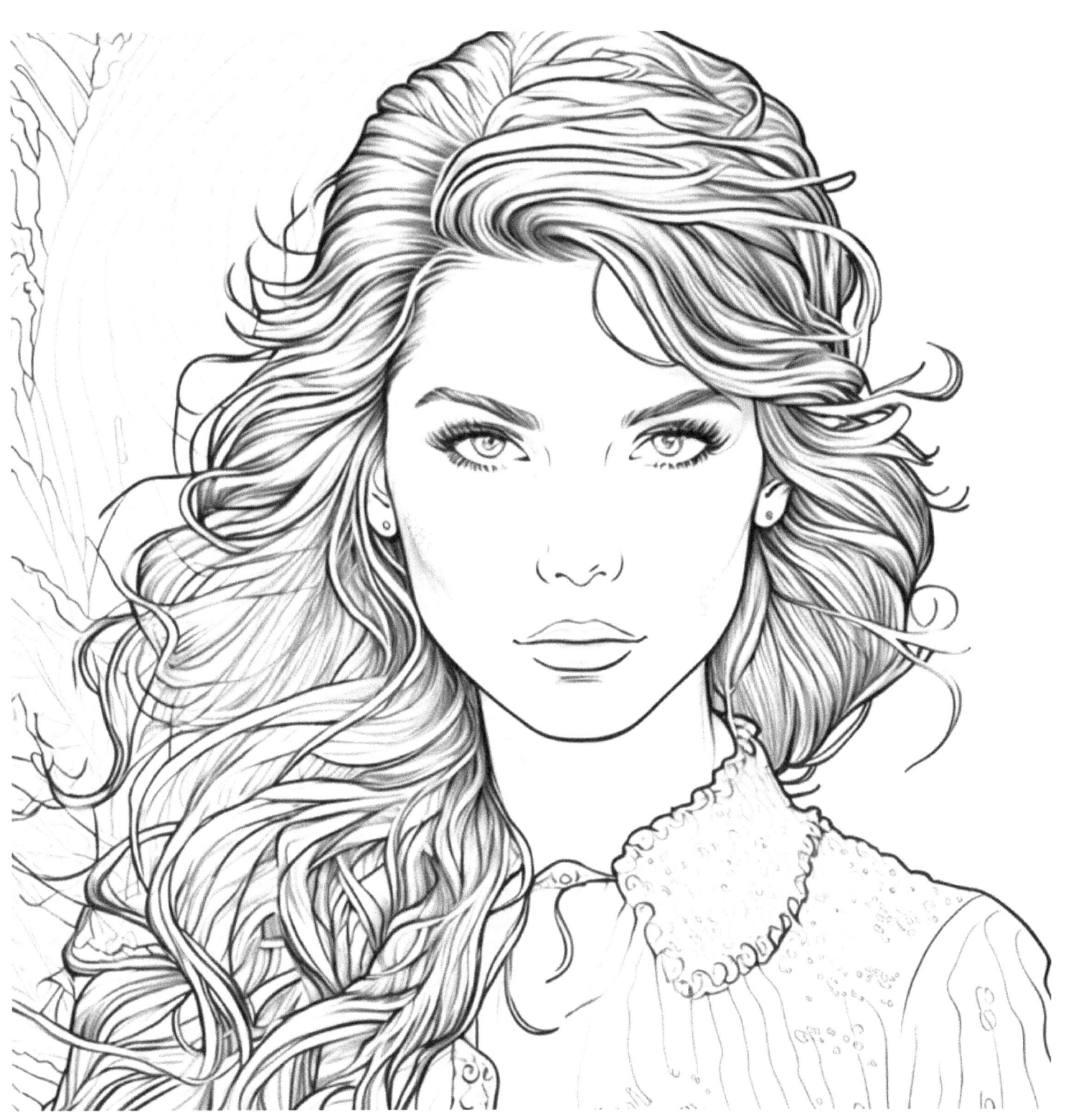

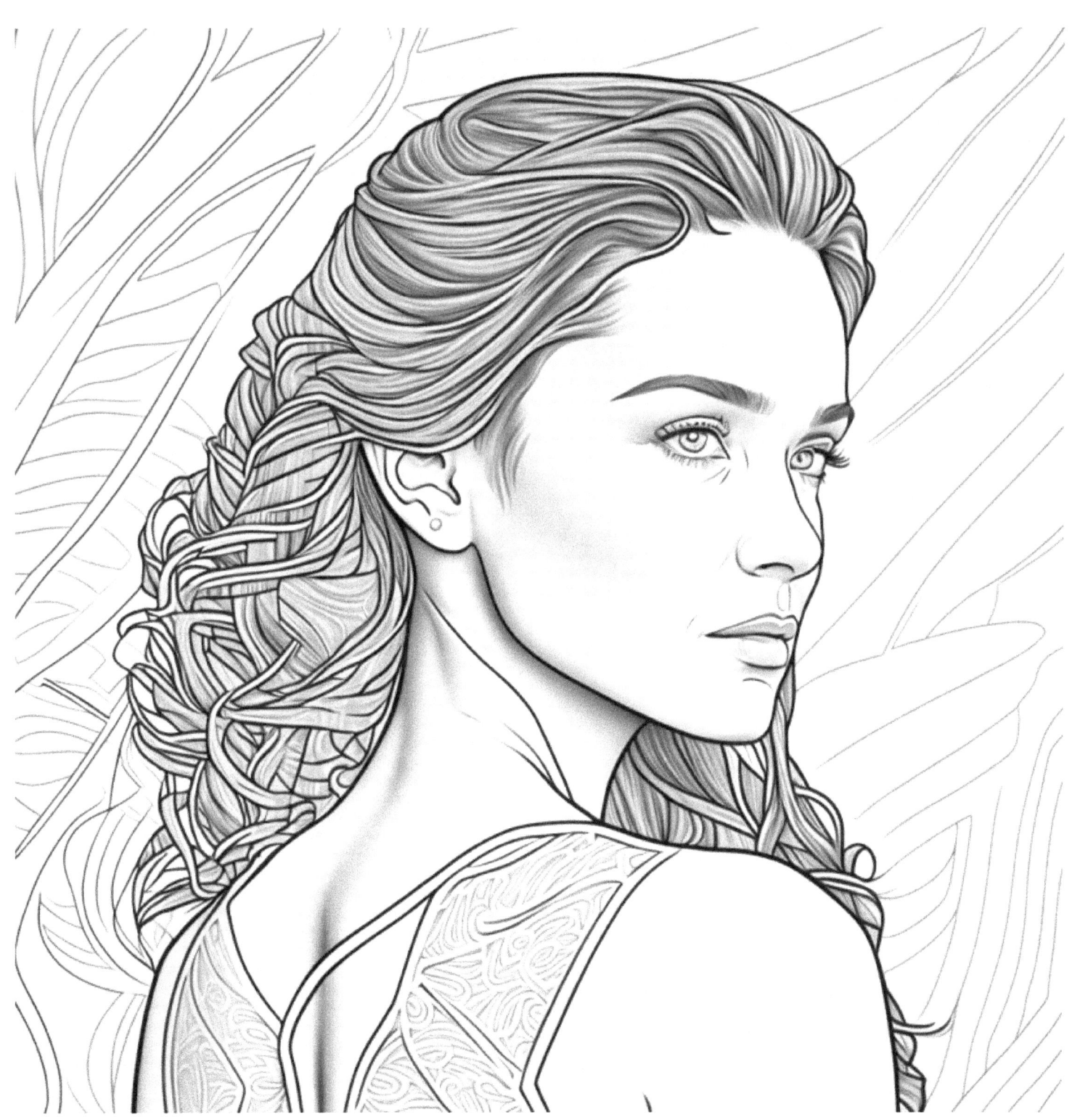

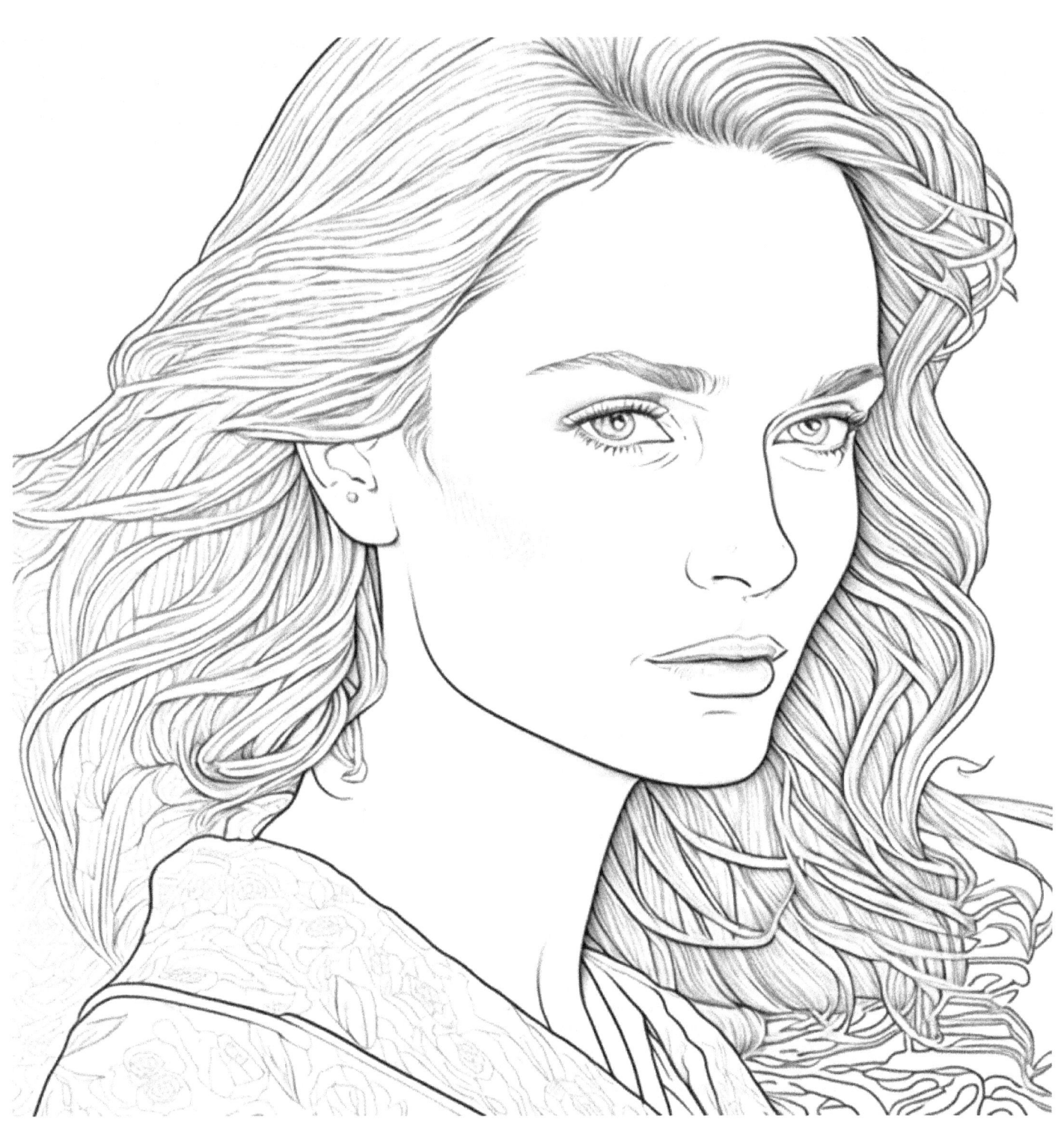

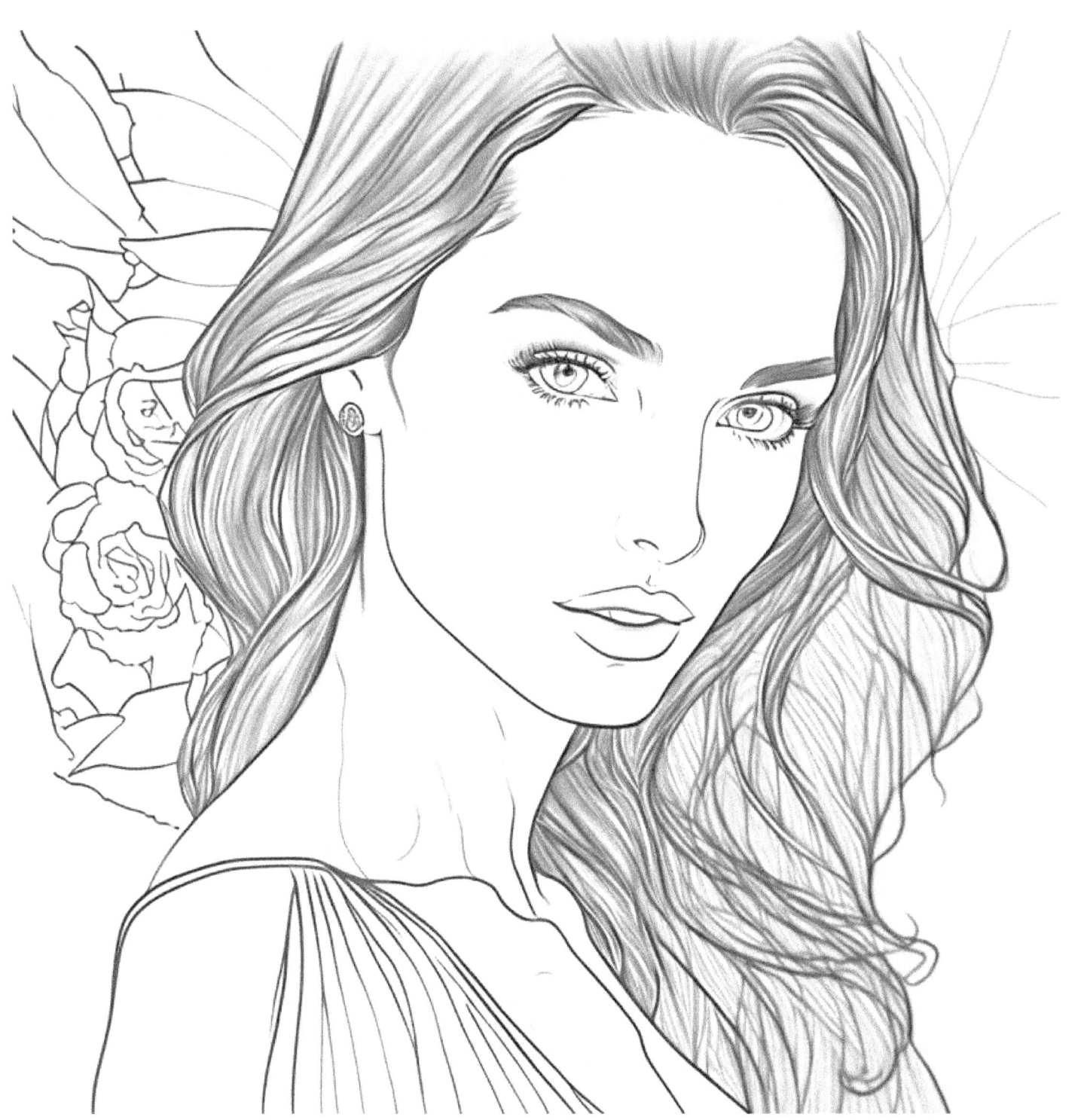

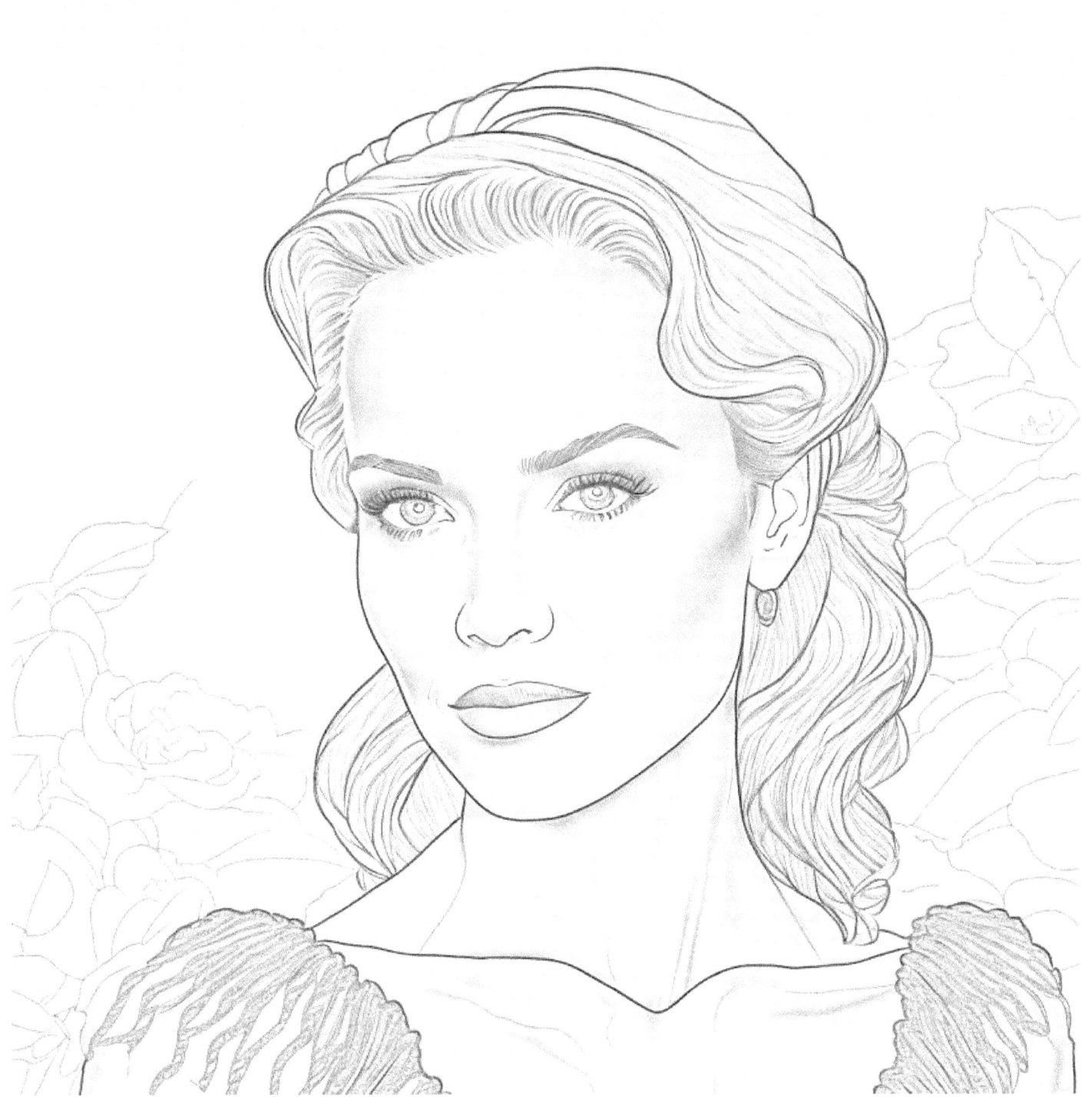

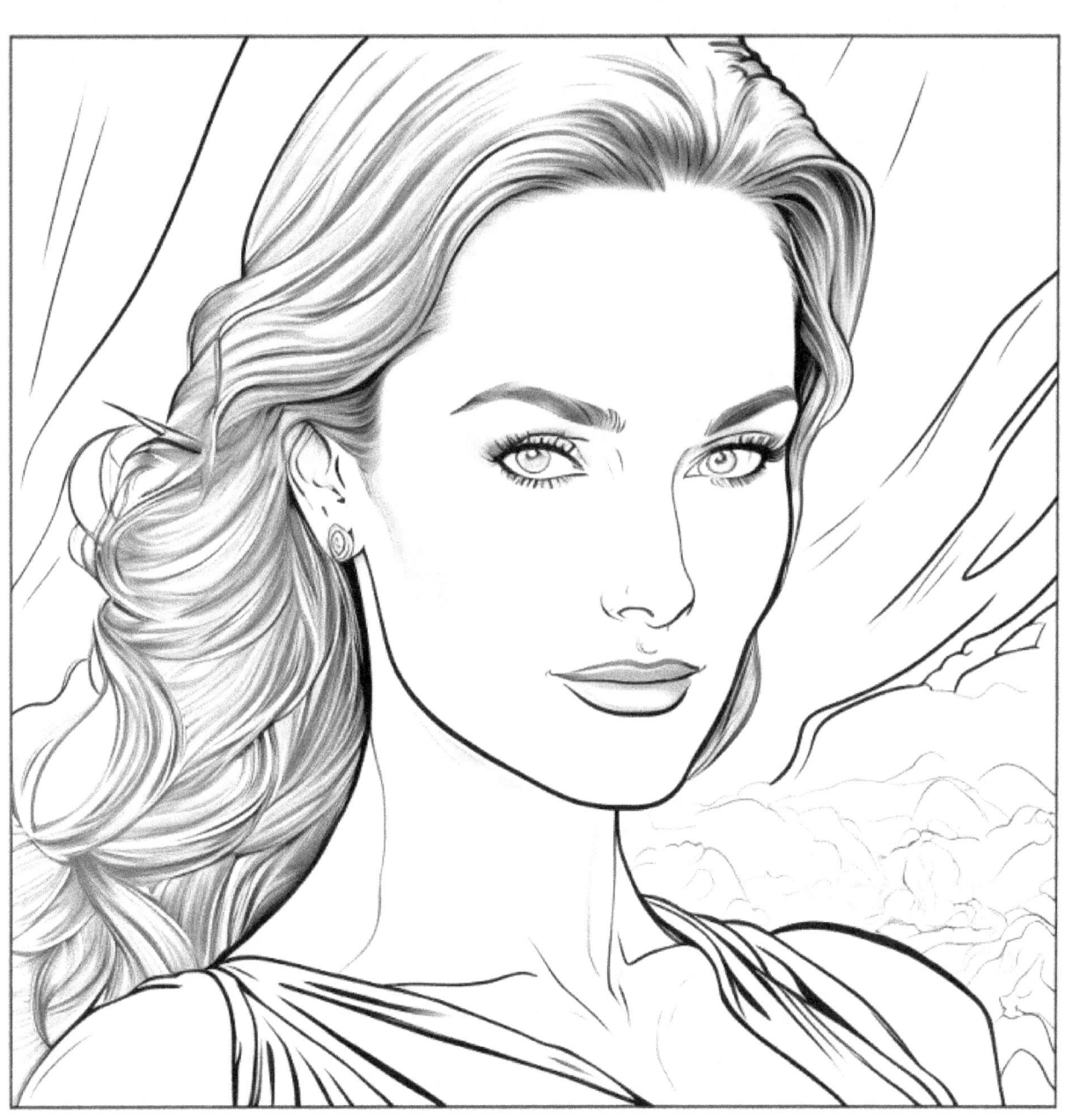

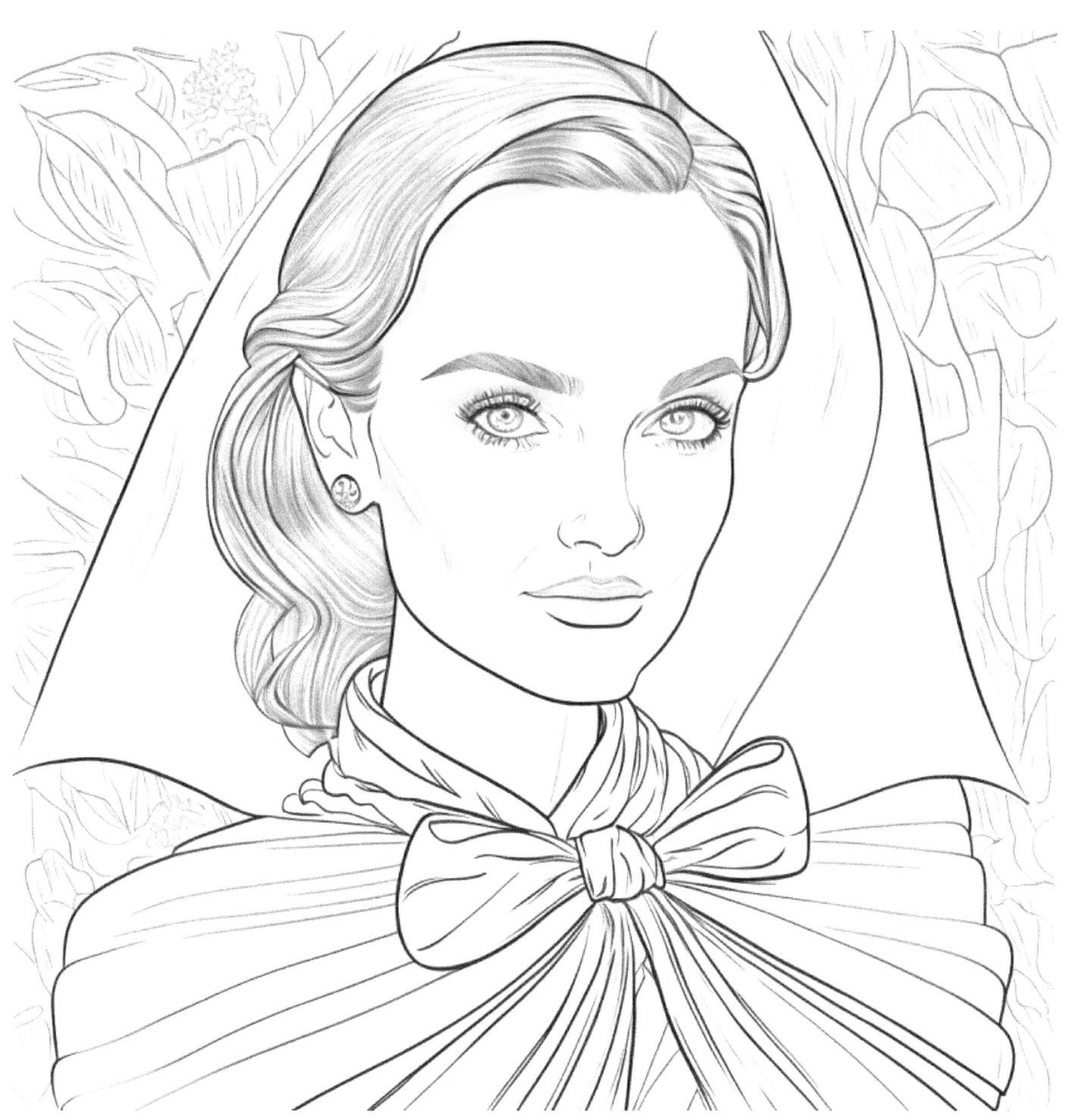

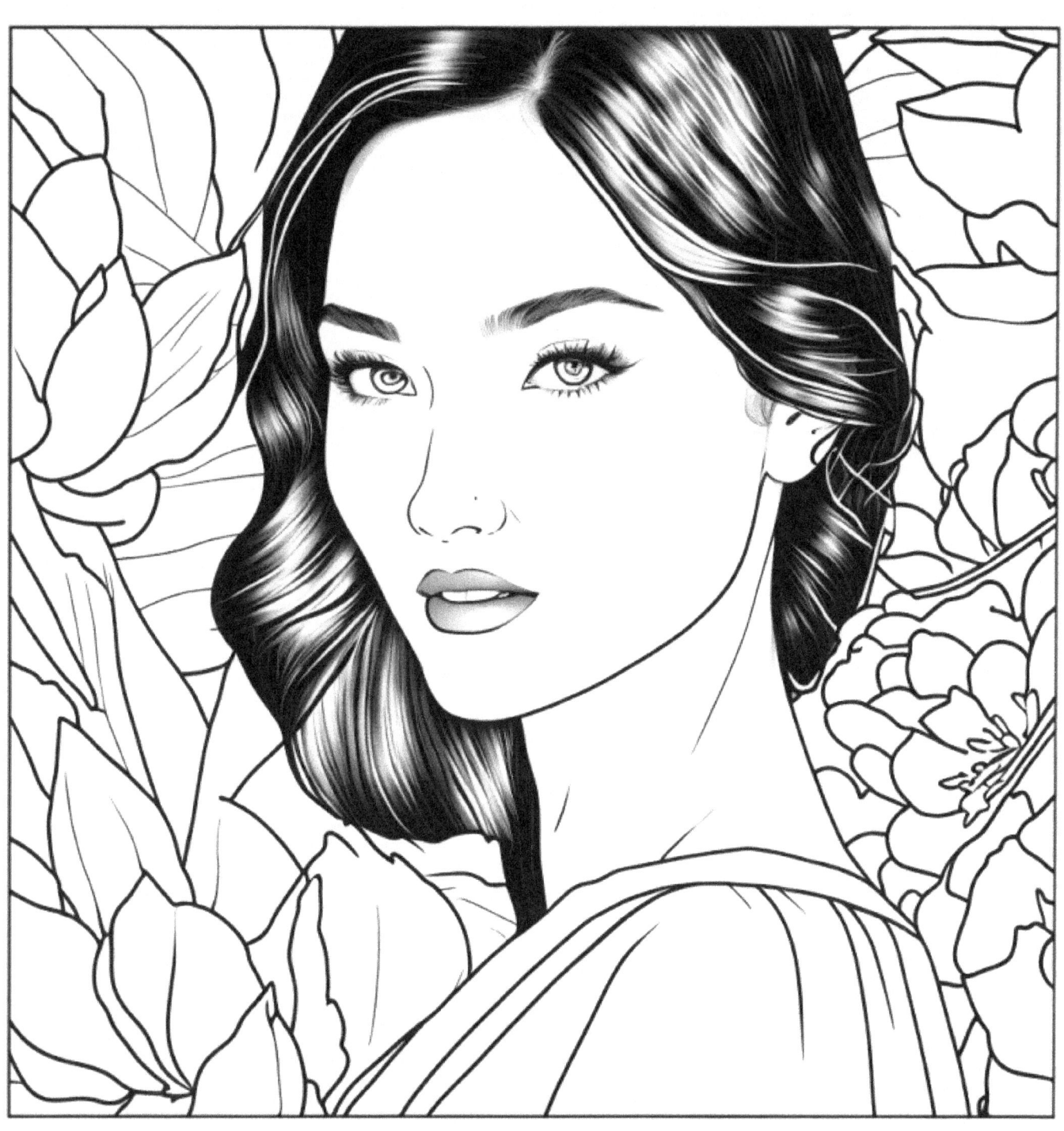

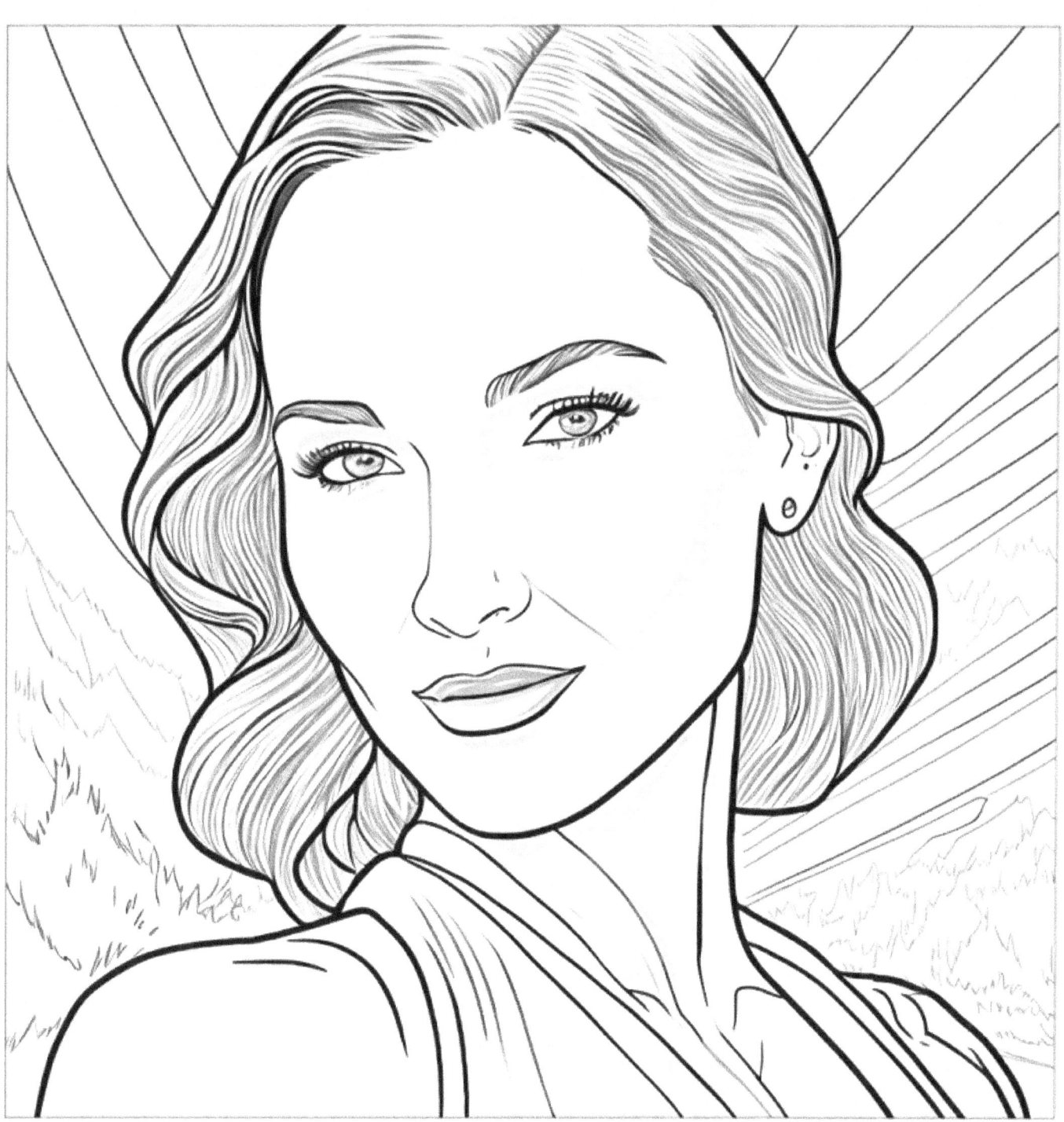

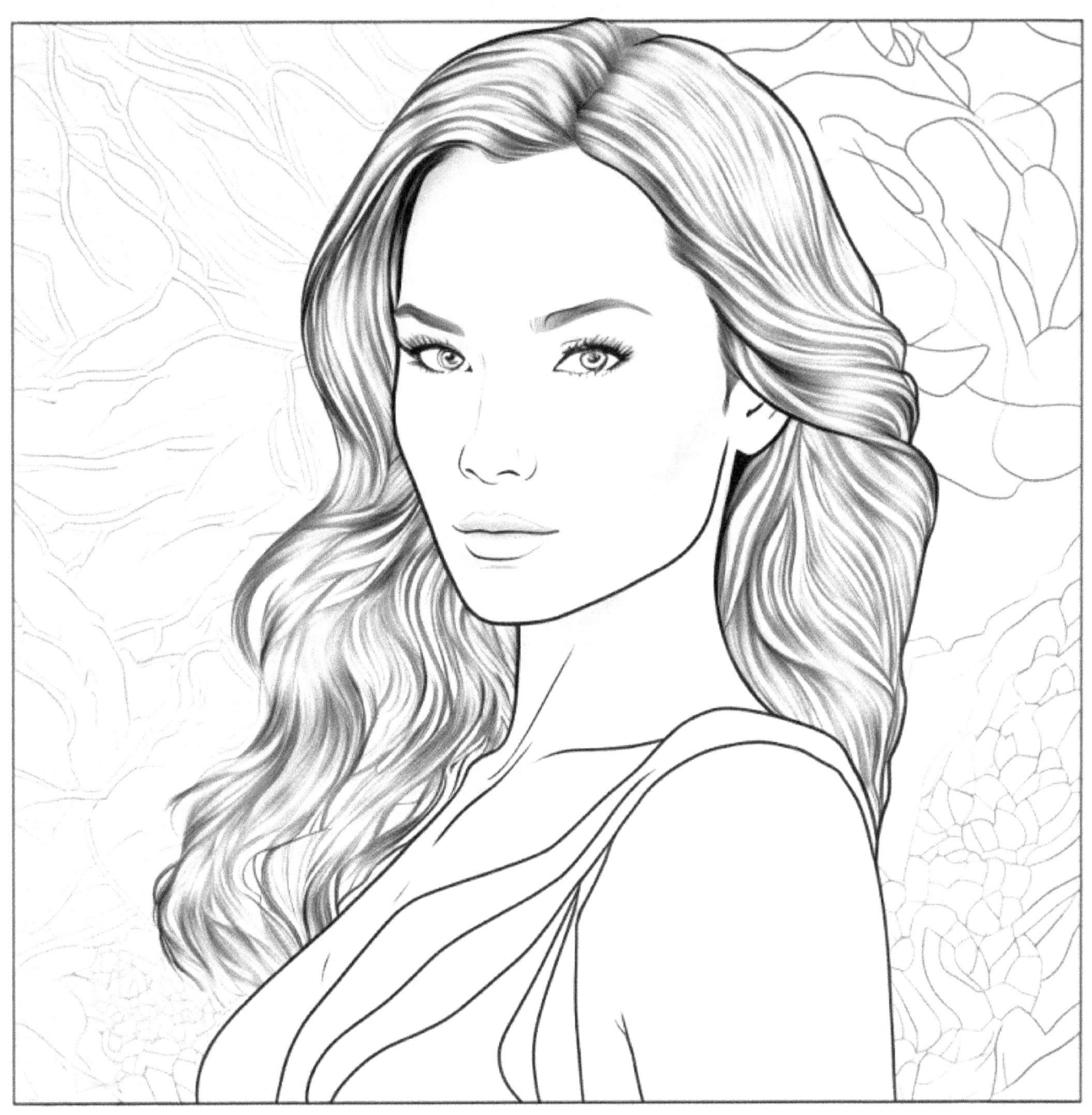

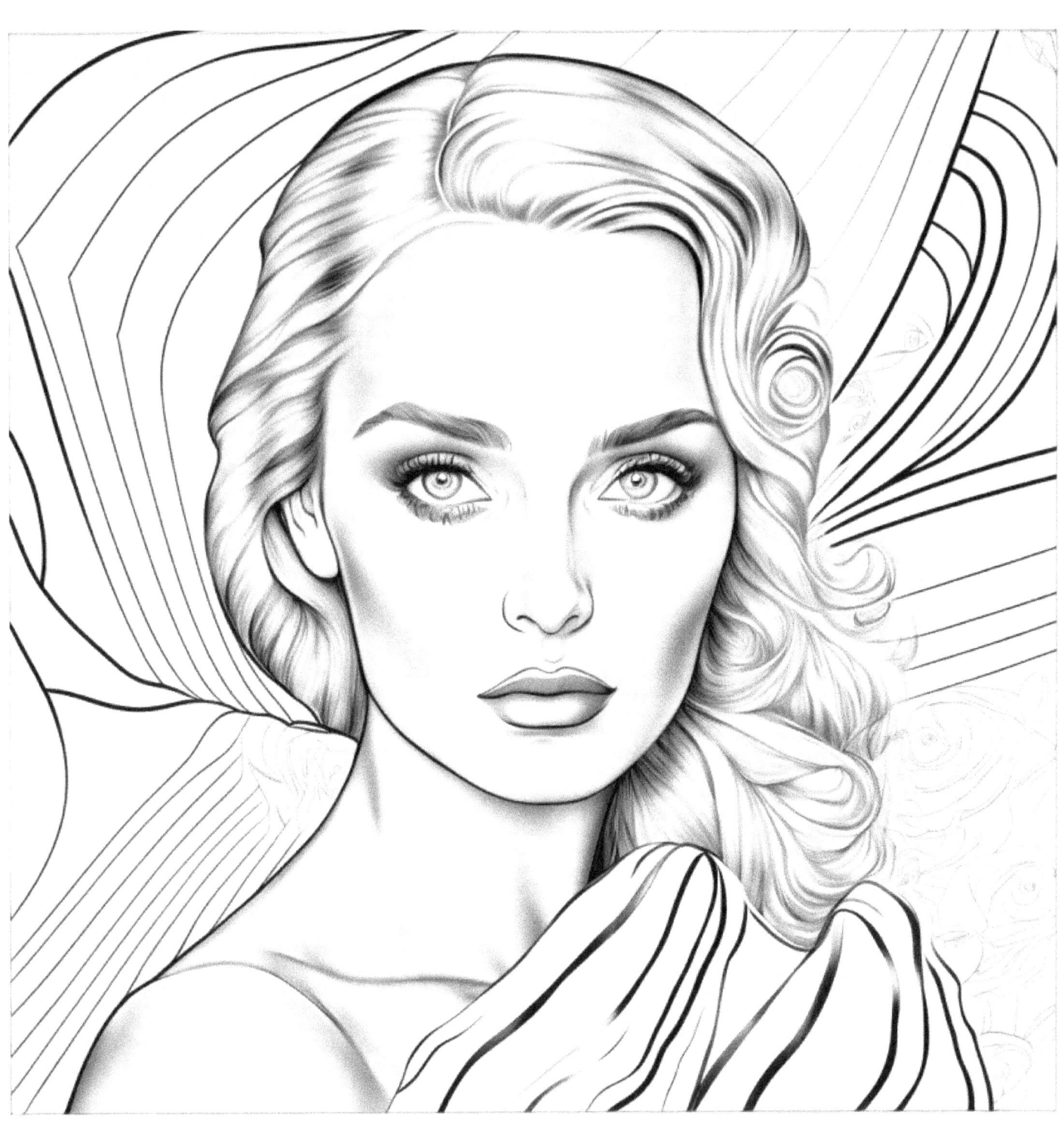

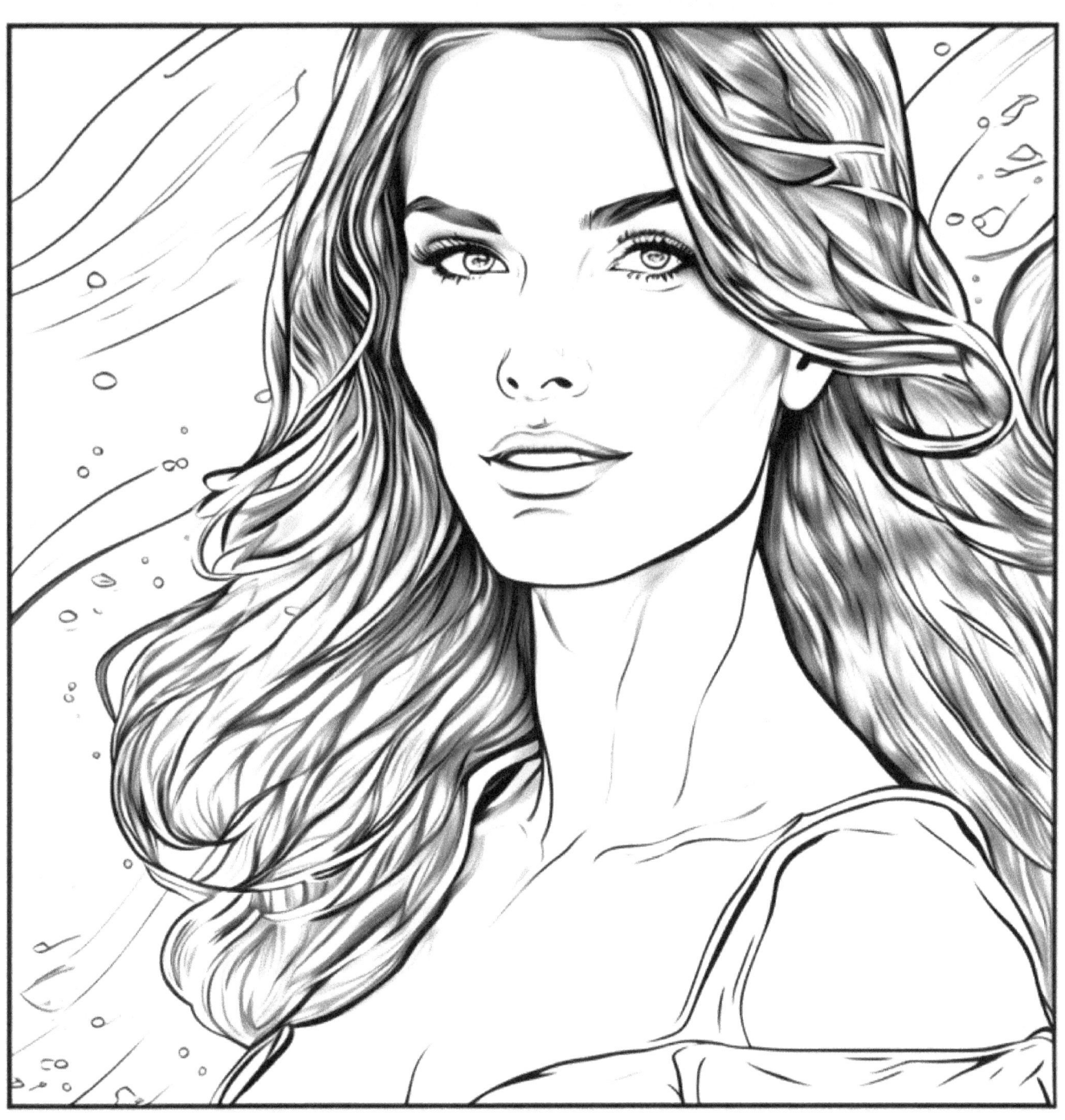

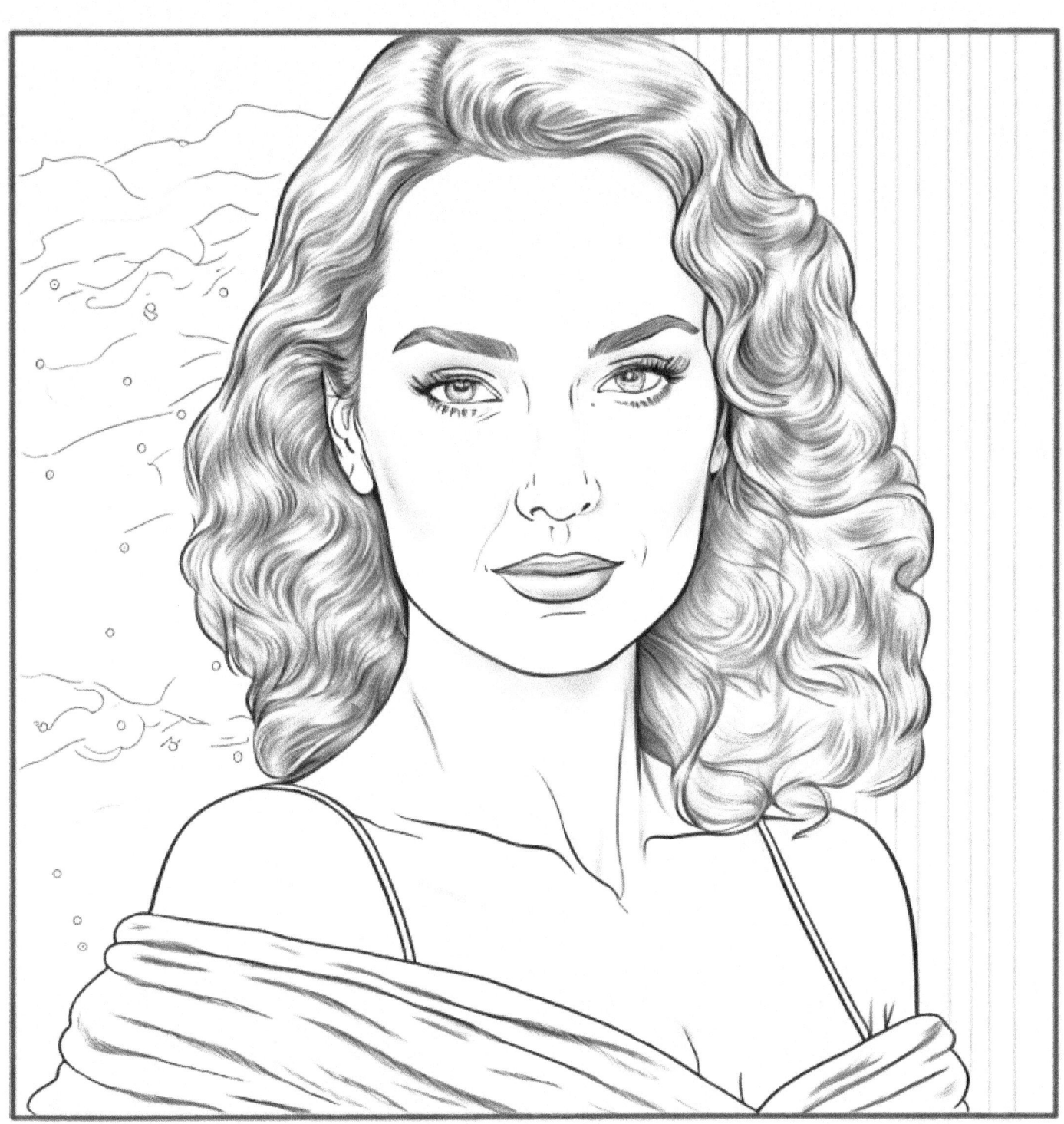